GREECE

TIME-LIFE BOOKS/AMSTERDAM

COOKERY AROUND THE WORLD
GREECE

KRISTINA LIKIDIS-KÖNIGSFELD

Food photography: Michael Brauner

Macedonia
(ex Yugoslavia)

Bulgaria

Albania

Macedonia

Thessaloniki

Chalkidiki

Corfu

Toannina

Mt.
Olympus

Epirus

Thessaly

Pelion

**Ionian
Islands**

N. Sporades

*Aege
Sea*

Levkas

Central Greece

Euboea

Kephalonia

Attica

Corinth

Peloponnese

Athens

Zakinthos

*Saronic
Gulf*

Cycl

*Ionian
Sea*

Kithira

Crete

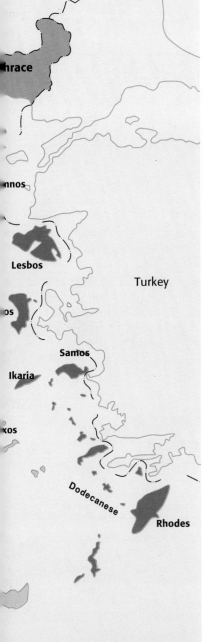

CONTENTS

Greece: Land of Sunshine and Hospitality _____ 7

Legacy of the Ancients _____ 9

   Thrace, Macedonia and the Chalkidiki Peninsula _____ 10

   Thessaly, Pelion Peninsula and Epirus _____ 12

   The Ionian Islands _____ 14

   Athens, Central Greece, Euboea and the Northern Sporades ___ 16

   The Peloponnese and the Islands of the Saronic Gulf _____ 18

   The Cyclades and Crete _____ 20

   Rhodes, the Dodecanese and the Northeast Aegean Islands ____ 22

Recipes _____ 25

   Starters and Salads _____ 25

   Soups _____ 47

   Pies _____ 55

   Eggs, Pasta and Rice _____ 67

   Fish and Seafood _____ 81

   Vegetables _____ 95

   Meat _____ 107

   Cakes and Pastries _____ 125

Suggested Menus _____ 138

   Glossary _____ 140

   Index _____ 143

GREECE: LAND OF SUNSHINE AND HOSPITALITY

Greece is a land of extraordinary beauty. The mainland, bounded by mountains on the north and west, is surrounded on three sides by sea. Its coast is an intricate pattern of inlets and rugged promontories, gulfs and peninsulas, natural harbours and long stretches of beach. The numerous islands, which make up approximately one fifth of the country's total landmass, are grouped or scattered throughout the Aegean Sea in the east and the Ionian Sea in the west. There are roughly 2,000 of these islands—ranging in size from over 8,000 square kilometres to little more than a rock jutting out of the water—but only about 170 are inhabited.

To most people, the very word Greece conjures up sundrenched coasts with picturesque villages of dazzling whitewashed houses, hills covered with olive groves, sandy coves beside the deep blue Aegean Sea and a friendly, hospitable people. A country steeped in history, its ancient sites are everywhere visible reminders that here Western civilization has its roots. This is the Greece that since time immemorial has cast its spell worldwide over painters, writers, archaeologists and travellers.

And what of the food? To the modern tourist, eating in hotel restaurants or village tavernas, true Greek cooking is not easy to find and the choice of local dishes may seem somewhat limited, but the Greeks love to eat well and have a tradition of good, simple food that reaches far back into antiquity. Every region has its own culinary preferences and specialities that have been handed down through generations.

Naturally, to enjoy a meal one must have the right ambience. Because the Greeks are a hospitable people, they love to invite both friends and strangers to join them in eating and drinking. To sit over a glass of ouzo or retsina, telling stories, laughing and savouring the food in convivial company is just as important to them as the food itself—whether the table is groaning under an array of *mezedes*, or appetizers, or the menu consists of deliciously fresh fish, charcoal-grilled kebabs, pasta or pies made of phyllo pastry and filled with vegetables, followed by a huge platter of juicy ripe seasonal fruit and sweet black Greek coffee.

During the 400-year-long Turkish occupation, the Orthodox Church became the guardian of tradition, and religious festivals, especially Easter, still continue to provide a welcome opportunity for sumptuous meals shared with family and friends. Outside the cities, everyday menus depend more on the time of year and local customs.

Spring marks the start of the season of imaginative vegetable dishes, lots of salads, and fresh fruit, ideal fare for the long, hot summer. Stews, pasta and fish predominate in the colder months. In the mountain areas are found game and cereal-based foods such as pies and noodles; on the fertile plains vegetables and fruit abound; while the coasts and islands offer a wide and plentiful variety of fresh fish and seafood. Grapes grow in profusion and each region takes pride in its own wines.

The first chapter of this book introduces the country and its people, some regional foods and specialities, as well as local wines and festivals. The recipe sections are divided according to the order in which dishes are served, starting with appetizers and soups and ending with desserts and pastries. Step photographs illustrate some of the more complicated techniques, and suggestions for variations or accompanying drinks are also included.

Finally, there are suggestions to help you plan Greek menus for different occasions and seasons, and a useful glossary of less familiar cooking terms and ingredients used in Greek cookery.

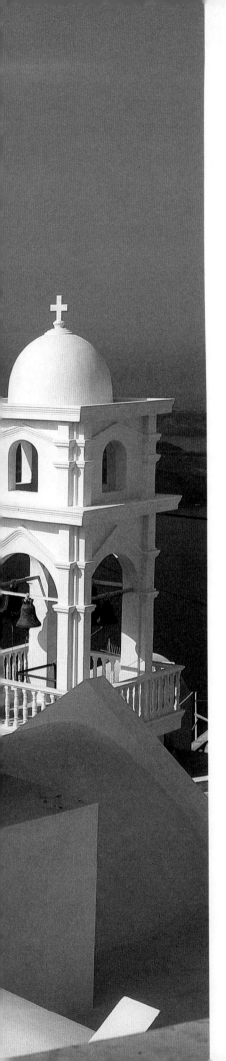

LEGACY OF THE ANCIENTS

Proud of their country and their ancient heritage, the Greek people of today are descended from such early civilizations as the Minoan and Cycladic in the south, and Indo-European migrants in the north and east. In the more remote areas, large communities grew up along the coasts of Asia Minor and around the Black Sea, communities that introduced grapevines, cereals, olive trees and many vegetables. In the eighth century BC, the time of Homer and the first Olympic Games, the Greeks founded colonies all round the Mediterranean, including southern Italy and Sicily.

Three hundred years later, Athens took over the leadership of the Greek states and defeated the threatening Persian Empire at the battle of Marathon. Thus began the so-called golden age of Athens. Under Pericles and a democratic rule, Greece flourished. This was an era of classical sculpture and architecture, and literature. After the death of Pericles in 429 BC, Athens began to lose control of Greece, first to the Spartans, then to Philip of Macedonia and his son Alexander the Great. At last, defeated by the Romans in 146 BC, Greece became a part of the Roman and later Byzantine empires and remained under foreign occupation for 1,900 years. Not until after the Greek war of liberation from the Turks in the 1820s did it become an independent country.

From the time of the classical era of the fifth century BC, Greek cooks were greatly respected for their skills. The importance of food and drink are evident not only in the writings of such men as Plato and Aristophanes but also in visual arts such as vase paintings—classical versions of comic-strips—depicting scenes of feasting and drinking. Both during the heyday of the Greek Empire and later under foreign rule, Greek cooking continued to flourish, and many of the Roman invaders took not only Greek art and culture but also their Greek cooks back with them to Rome.

Because of changing geographical boundaries and historic links with Asia Minor, Byzantium, Italy and the city state of Venice, Greek cooking absorbed a range of influences, seen in many dishes today. Some dishes with Turkish names gave rise to the belief that much Greek cuisine was introduced by the Turks; in fact, the names were mandatory during the Turkish occupation, and such dishes were found throughout the Mediterranean area.

If legend is correct, however, Greece gave the Western world its most distinctive cookery insignia: during the Middle Ages, Greek cooks in the monasteries wore tall white hats to distinguish them from the black ones worn by the monks; these are said to be the origin of the familiar chef's hat.

A peasant milks his goats on the Chalkidiki peninsula. Lying south of Thessaloniki, the three-pronged peninsula reaching out into the Aegean is fast becoming a popular holiday resort.

Thrace, Macedonia and the Chalkidiki Peninsula

The northern Greek provinces of Thrace and Macedonia, bordering Turkey, Bulgaria, former Yugoslavia and Albania, have a turbulent frontier history, as might be expected. But between the forest-clad mountains and the Aegean, the fertile plains and river valleys include some of the most productive agricultural land in the whole country. Fruit and vegetables abound and among the major food crops are cereals and grapes.

Thrace

Thrace, the northeastern tip of Greece, separated from Turkey in the east by the River Evros, forms a link between Europe and Asia. The course of the Via Egnatia, the ancient Roman route to Byzantium (now Istanbul) on the Bosphorus, has scarcely changed. Steep slopes are covered with pine and fir forests. In the valleys and plains between the crystalline Rhodope massif on the Bulgarian border and the lagoons of the Aegean Sea, crops include tobacco, cotton, maize, olives

and grapes. The climate is more Balkan than Mediterranean and the architecture in cities such as Komotini and Xanthi, centre of the tobacco industry, shows eastern influences.

The province is part of a historical region named after the peoples who settled the area in about 2000 BC. Formerly part-Turkish, part-Bulgarian, western Thrace was ceded to Greece at the Treaty of Sèvres in 1920. The subsequent massive exchange of populations meant many Anatolian Greek refugees arrived in the area from Turkey, bringing with them their religious and culinary traditions, evident in the monasteries and village minarets of the minority Muslim communities and in the Oriental fragrances pervading the local cuisine.

Specialities of Xanthi include *revani,* or semolina cake, and *kourabiedes,* or almond shortbread. Locals and travellers alike enjoy the famous coffee of Komotini, whose pungent and tempting aroma wafts into the streets each morning. In these narrow, old-town streets, craftsmen hammer out little copper pots used for brewing mocha. Another speciality of the region is *loukanika,* spicy sausages sold on Tuesdays at the weekly market. At Agia Eleni and Aglos Petros, near Seres, the festival of St. Constantine and St. Helena is celebrated on May 21 with processions and folk dancing. In July, there is a wine festival in Alexandroupolis.

Macedonia

Across the River Nestos to the west of Thrace, Macedonia, once the kingdom of Philip and Alexander, is the largest, most prosperous of the Greek provinces. Strawberries, peaches, apples and numerous fresh vegetables thrive here. In the early morning in Kavalla harbour, the silver fish sparkle in their damp baskets. Quayside stalls are laden with prawns, mackerel, red mullet, squid and octopus. In the backstreet markets, peasant women sell bundles of herbs, fresh vegetables, blocks of cheese, sacks of pulses and *trahana*, a dried mixture of wheat and yogurt used for making soup. From Kavalla's lively port, ferries sail for the islands of Samothrace and Thasos, famous for its wines and white marble and venue of a classical drama and music festival every July and August.

Thessaloniki, the provincial capital, is a city rich in history and full of levantine charm. It has a reputation for excellent fish and seafood dishes, such as *midia tiganita*, deep-fried mussels. Among the best of the Macedonian red wines are the strong, dry Naoussa and the medium, oak-aged Goumenissa.

The Demetriada arts festival is held in October in Thessaloniki. At nearby Langada, the feast of St. Constantine and St. Helena on May 21 is marked by an ancient rite of pagan origin: fire-walkers bearing holy icons dance barefoot over red-hot coals, to the clash of tambourines.

Chalkidiki Peninsula

At the eastern prong of the Chalkidiki peninsula is the independent monastic republic of Athos, still forbidden to women. Once the spiritual centre of the Greek Orthodox Church, it now has fewer than 20 monasteries, but the population of some 2,000 monks are still masters at making the traditional red Athos wine from cabernet grapes.

The other two slender promontories, Kassandra and Sithonia, like the neighbouring island of Thasos, are popular holiday destinations. The Sithonia vineyards produce fruity, high-quality red and white wines under the appellation Côtes de Meliton.

The turquoise water and long, sweeping beaches of the Kassandra peninsula are a haven for holidaymakers.

A fishing boat lies peacefully at anchor in Neos Marmaras harbour on Sithonia.

Thessaly, Pelion Peninsula and Epirus

Three parallel mountain ranges sweep down across the Greek mainland in a southeasterly direction. The huge Pindos range, which dominates the interior, is flanked to the west by the mountains of Epirus rising up in the hinterland of the Ionian coastline, and to the east by the majestic Olympus massif, whose highest peak, 2,917-metre Mount Olympus, dominates the plain of Thessaly. Farther south, the Pelion mountain range sits on its own little peninsula.

Thessaly

The plain of Thessaly, the bread-basket of Greece, lies between the towns of Larissa, Volos and Karditsa. Mountain rivers supply water for the crops and feed the many reservoirs.

Thessaly is a land of myths. Mount Olympus, towering above the plains and visible from the sea to the east, was believed the home of the Greek gods. Jason and his Argonauts set out from Iolkos, on the Gulf of Volos, in search of the Golden Fleece. And the ancient healing springs at Trikala are a reminder that here the cult of Asklepios, god of healing, has its roots.

In the west, where the plain ends and the Pindos Mountains begin, nature has fashioned an extraordinary phenomenon—the mighty crags of Meteora (*opposite page, top*). On their barren peaks, 500 metres above the valley (*meteoros* means "high in the air"), stand a dozen or so monasteries, the remaining bulwarks of Orthodox Christianity against Turkish and Albanian invaders.

Along the rugged Aegean coast near Volos there are still good catches of fish and seafood. A typical local dish is *oktapodi stifado*, octopus baked

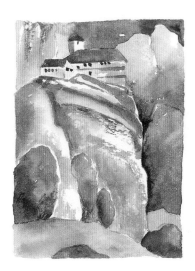

with lots of small onions, tomatoes, cinnamon and wine. Another local dish, *spetsofai*, consists of eggs on a bed of vegetables cooked in a clay pot with tomatoes, peppers, little sausages, wine and cheese, and is traditionally accompanied by retsina from nearby Nea Anhialos, where an annual wine festival is held in August. At Agria there is a fishermen's festival in early July.

Pelion Peninsula

Forested Mount Pelion, the focus of this lovely peninsula, once was said to be the home of the half-man half-horse centaurs. Later, the region was famous for its silk industry which brought the people a measure of prosperity. This declined, as did the economy, but many of the old village houses have recently been restored, and these dignified mountain villages are among the most beautiful in Greece. Visitors rambling through the idyllic Pelion mountains can admire more than 200 different varieties of wild flowers and medicinal herbs growing on the slopes.

Epirus

Once almost entirely inaccessible to the outside world, the towns and villages around the Epirus Mountains on the Ionian Sea remained long independent. Even under Turkish domination, upland areas and towns such as Ioannina retained a measure of autonomy. Made affluent through trading in wool, they became lively cultural centres. And they created their own imaginative cuisine based on locally grown produce.

Mountain villages with Epirus-style buildings are well worth a detour. Their friendly inhabitants are famous both for their handicrafts and for their pies. Southwest of Ioannina is the ancient oracle of Zeus at Dodona, once a sacred oak tree where the rustling of the leaves was interpreted by the priests.

On the island in the lake at Ioannina, café owners take special pride in serving a local delicacy, crayfish simmered with oil, lemon and oregano, or fried and served with *skordalia*, a garlic purée. Trout from the clear mountain streams, wild boar, hare and rabbit are also prepared in delicious ways.

In Epirus there are as many as 30 different variations of pitta bread filled with meat, cheese, spinach or wild vegetables and cooked in a *tapsi,* a round, high-sided tin pan. Local cheeses, such as hard and piquant *metsovone kapnisto* or *formano*, mild *manouri*, or fresh-tasting *mitzithra* are favourites on a picnic. *Vissino glyko*, cherries or other fruit preserved in syrup, are also popular.

The best local wines include Katoi from Metsovo and the white wines of Zitsa, though production is limited and they are hard to find outside the region.

For peasants living in remote mountain areas, the donkey is still the most important means of transport.

A rural, pink-washed house near Agios Gordios nestles in a picturesque hillside of western Corfu. The most northern of the Ionian Islands, Corfu is also the most popular.

The Ionian Islands

With their Renaissance façades and delicate campanili, or bell towers, the Ionian Islands have an undeniably Italian air. This is hardly surprising, since the Eptanisos ("seven islands") were under Venetian rule for 400 years; with the exception of Levkas, they were never under Turkish jurisdiction. When the Venetians withdrew in 1797, the islands became successively Italian, French, briefly Russian and, in 1815, British protectorates. Not until 1864 did Britain return them to Greece.

These islands do not share the bleakness of many of their sister islands in the Aegean or elsewhere in the Mediterranean. With their lush, almost tropical, vegetation they look like specks of green scattered across the blue Ionian Sea. Corfu, the most northerly island, is close to Albania, Levkas is close to the Greek mainland, while the most southerly, Kithira, is at

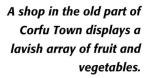

A shop in the old part of Corfu Town displays a lavish array of fruit and vegetables.

the southern tip of the Peloponnese.

The fun-loving nature of the island-dwellers is clear to see in their brightly-coloured regional costumes and their delight at celebrating their various festivals. The cuisine of the different islands has much in common. Pasta, popular throughout Greece, is a special favourite on the Ionian Islands, especially when prepared with onions and tomatoes or meat, or with mussels Italian-style. The range of sweetmeats shows both east and west influences. *Mandolata*, a white almond sweet, can be found in pastry shops, while village bakeries make *galactobouriko*, a fragrant, enticing tart with creamy semolina and butter. Kumquat liqueur is an ideal souvenir of the islands.

When it comes to wine there is fierce competition. Each island takes pride in its own product, though most of the wines are made from the same local grape varieties. The mountainous terrain of the islands provides little space for vineyards, so the vines are cultivated on terraces.

Corfu

Almost half the population of the whole archipelago lives on Corfu. With its neo-classic and Italian-style buildings, its colonnaded arcades, elegant pavement cafés and the Esplanade—once a Venetian parade ground—Corfu is a mixture of cosmopolitan sophistication and relaxed Greek simplicity. But the food on the island, especially in the mountain villages, is with few exceptions unmistakably Greek.

The rest of the Mediterranean has the Greeks to thank for its olive trees. On Corfu, however, they were first planted by the Venetians, and the

olive groves have now become veritable forests. Corfu's temperate climate also produces fine fruit and vegetables, which the Corfiotes like to combine with meat or fish. The local *stifado*, for example, is a meat stew with quinces.

Like the rest of the Ionians, Corfiotes love festivities. Whatever the occasion, everyone joins in with equal gusto, whether it is a procession in honour of St. Spiridon, patron saint of Corfu, whose image is paraded through Corfu Town in Easter Week and on August 1, or Carnival in Levkimi in the south.

Levkas and Kephalonia

The people of Levkas, the only Ionian island to have been occupied by the Turks, are partial to pungent flavours. The garlic and potato paste, *Skordalia*, here made with almonds, is a popular accompaniment to grilled fish. The dark local wine is affectionately known as Santa Mavra—"blessed black".

The island of Kephalonia is the home of dry Robola wine, thought by many to be Greece's finest white wine. Muscatel grapes give fruitiness and sweetness to the dark red Mavrodaphne. There is also thyme honey from the mountains and *kidonopasto*, quince paste.

Cultural highlights include the drama festival at Argostoli in July, the Feast of the Assumption at Assos and Lixuri on August 15, and the procession of sacred relics at the monastery of Agios Gerassimos on August 16. Folk dance festivals are held at Argostoli and Lixuri in early September.

Ithaca, Zakinthos and Kithira

Flanking Kephalonia to the east is Ithaca, the legendary home of Odysseus. Inland, the air is fragrant with herbs and flowering shrubs. Many families still press their own wine.

Zakinthos, or Zante, lives up to its name of *fior di Levante*, flower of the Levant, with a profusion of spring flowers, good local wines and Fraoula, a strawberry liqueur with a floral aroma. Rocky Kithira, the southernmost island in the Ionian Sea, was once a major centre of worship of Aphrodite, goddess of love, and is renowned, appropriately enough, for its honey.

A Greek Orthodox priest walks from the church at Levkimi in the southernmost part of Corfu. Orthodox priests still wield considerable influence among the island's communities.

Six draped women, or caryatids, support the roof of the south portico of the Erechtheion, an Ionic temple on the Akropolis in Athens. Because the temple served several cults, its design included three porches and three different floor levels.

This towering rock door on Skiathos is reached by taking a boat from Lalaria beach.

Athens, Central Greece, Euboea and the Northern Sporades

Athens

Dominated by the Akropolis and a focal point of Greek history for 3,000 years, Athens is where the ancient and modern world meet most forcibly. The first-time visitor may find it hard to reconcile today's traffic-ridden urban sprawl with the monuments of antiquity, but this many-faceted capital has more to offer than its history.

For example, there are the markets. South of Omonia Square is the famous meat and fish market. Whole lambs dangle next to sides of beef, chickens, hares and huge lumps of liver. Using a cleaver on a wooden chopping block, the butcher prepares meat according to customers' wishes. Round the sides, huge pots of *patsas* bubble away—a soup for strong stomachs, including

offal, and lamb's head and feet.

In the fish hall, a colourful diversity of fresh fish and seafood is loaded onto counters; because local catches are less plentiful, they are supplemented by deep-frozen sole, swordfish and spiny lobsters from distant fishing grounds.

The narrow streets surrounding the market are crowded with shops and stalls offering vegetables, cheese, salt cod, herbs, fruits preserved in syrup, toasted walnuts, chick-peas and baskets full of *koulouria*, or sesame seed rings. One's nose is kept busy tracking down the many stalls cooking a variety of traditional fast foods such as *souvlakia*, grilled meat on skewers.

The old city beneath the Acropolis comes to life in the evenings and this part of Athens takes on an almost village atmosphere. At the rickety tables of the little tavernas, Athenians tuck into prawns with feta cheese, stuffed vine leaves and squid. Those who do not drink ouzo wash the meal down with red or white retsina. Since antiquity, this wine, with its potent taste of resin, has been produced exclusively in Greece. In ancient times, pine resin from the forests round Athens was added to the must before or during fermentation in order to preserve the wine. Now drinkers simply like the taste.

The Greek Orthodox Easter in Athens, when thousands take part in the candle-lit processions, is an unforgettable experience. At midnight, they serve *mayiritsa*, a soup made from lamb's offal. Another traditional fare at Easter is red-coloured hard-boiled eggs.

Piraeus, a major freight and liner port as well as a ferry link between Athens and the islands, is a bustling, lively town. Every January 6, during the Epiphany celebrations, the Archbishop of Piraeus throws a cross into the sea to bless the waters. At Daphni, 13 kilometres from Athens, a wine festival, at which visitors can taste wines from all over Greece, is held between the end of June and the end of September.

Central Greece

The region stretching from the Aegean to the Ionian Sea is a land of mountains, forests, lakes and pastures, and a coastline that gently rolls, or precipitously plunges, into the sea. From Thebes, home of Oedipus, and the Pass of Thermopylae, where the Spartans stood fast against the Persians, to the ancient oracle at Delphi, the region is steeped in history.

In village and town alike, ancient customs are lovingly preserved, and Easter is celebrated with special

fervour. It is also a major wine-growing area; Mavroudi, a red wine from Delphi, is dark and fruity. Goat's cheese and butter are specialities of the region. The melodious tinkle of cow and sheep bells fills the air around the workshops of Karpenissi, where they are made.

Euboea and Northern Sporades

When they tire of city life, Athenians head for the island of Euboea, which keeps the capital supplied with wine, olives, figs, grain, nuts, honey and meat and, most important, walnuts—for the Athenian nut cake, *karidopitta*.

To the northeast are the Northern Sporades—Skiathos, Skopelos, Alonissis and Skiros plus a few smaller ones. In summer the beaches here are crowded with bathers and the harbours filled with yachts, but the scenery is delightful and there is always something new to discover in the tradition-steeped towns and villages. Some of the islands also have a thriving agriculture. Skopelos, for example, has extensive plum orchards and almond groves. Skiros offers juicy figs and citrus fruits. Fish served in any waterside taverna tastes delicious seasoned with island-grown thyme, sage and oregano.

A tempting selection of nuts, dried fruit, spices and sweetmeats draws potential customers into this Athens shop. The city's bustling food markets are a feast for the eyes as well as the stomach.

Two Evzones guard the Tomb of the Unknown Soldier in Athens. These soldiers, wearing traditional uniforms resembling the Greek national costume, belong to a unit with a 170-year history whose duties are mainly ceremonial.

Sesame seeds and honey make a delicious sweetmeat which can be bought on practically any street corner.

The Peloponnese and the Islands of the Saronic Gulf

The Peloponnese

Since the Corinth Canal cuts through the only strip of land that joins it to the Greek mainland, the Peloponnese is more an island than a peninsula. And like an island it has an independent way of life.

Populated since the early Stone Age, it is rich in ancient sites and mythology. From here the Greeks set sail to fight the Trojan War after the abduction of Helen of Sparta. At Mycenae, mythic seat of King Agamemnon and his treacherous wife Clytemnestra, archaeologists have unearthed many spectacular treasures. At Epidaurus, site of a sanctuary of Asklepios and a major healing centre, there are still performances in the magnificent fourth-century BC theatre, with its perfect acoustics and a seating capacity of 14,000. And the Olympic Games originated at the sanctuary of Olympia on the west side of the peninsula.

The ancient division into seven administrative regions is more or less unchanged. Each province has its own special character. The country is predominantly mountainous and the central uplands of Arcadia, with its olive groves, picturesque market towns, idyllic scenery and Mount Erimanthos, at 2,224 metres the peninsula's highest peak, is still relatively remote. Achaea, in the north, is famous for its wines, and Patras is the peninsula's main commercial port.

Corinth in the northeast, with its citrus plantations and vineyards, is the only land link with Athens via the Corinth Canal bridge. Dried currants are said to have originated here. According to legend, nobody in Corinth remembered to pick the grapes, which then dried, withered and turned black. Subsequently, Venetians returning home from Greece sampled the shrivelled fruit and liked their slightly peppery sweetness; so the Corinthians promptly established a thriving export trade. In the autumn, carpets of grapes laid out to dry can be seen everywhere.

Farther east are the olive groves of Argolis, where fields of sunflowers, artichokes and cereal crops, apricots and vineyards also flourish. Waving fields of grain grow on the Laconian plain in the southeast, once home to the Spartans. On its western border, the lofty 100-kilometre-long Taygetos range divides it from Messenia, famous for plump Kalamata olives and black figs. And farther north, in Ilia, with Olympia nestling in the gentle hills at the foot of Mount Kronos, there are stretches of golden sandy beaches and low-lying fields of wheat and maize.

Village life in the Peloponnese proceeds at a leisurely pace. In high summer it is good to sit under the centuries-old plane trees, drinking coffee and chatting. The arrival of a bus-load of tourists has little effect, except on the owner of the taverna and the souvenir seller.

Small low walls; fields of dazzling red poppies; herds of sheep and goats; and the shepherds' little stone refuges—a journey through the mountains and valleys offers a succession of charming scenes. In the fishing ports, octopuses hang out to dry like washing in the blazing sun. Under an arbour of vines, you can enjoy grilled fish, a salad of wild vegetables with ewe's cheese

and olives, and the local wine.

Fifty per cent of Greece's vineyards are in the Peloponnese, most along the hilly coasts of the Gulf of Corinth and the Ionian Sea, but also a few at higher altitudes. Red Mavrodaphne from the Patras area is sweet and dark, the whites and rosés are pleasantly refreshing. The dry red and white Demesticas also come from here. From the eastern Nemea district, 200 to 800 metres above sea level, come forceful dark reds. In contrast, at 650 metres in Arcadia, Mantinia produces a light, flowery, dry white wine.

The Peloponnese are a hospitable people who are happy for outsiders to join in their festivals. At Leonidio on the coast, carnival is celebrated in February, while Easter is marked by the ceremonial burning of an effigy of Judas, to the crackle of fireworks. To eat, there is lamb roasted on a spit, and sweet pastries like *galaktobouriko*, a delicious custard pie.

Saronic Islands

A handful of small islands including Salamis, Aegina and Poros lie in the Saronic Gulf between Attica and the Peloponnese. Close to the coast of Argolis are the islands of Hydra and Spetses. These enchanting places attract both Athenians and tourists.

Aegina is famous for its Temple of Aphaia and its pink-blossomed pistachio nut trees. Aegina Town has a lively harbour. Only a stone's thrown from Piraeus, Salamis—scene of a decisive sea battle against the Persians in 480 BC—lures many visitors to its beautiful sandy beaches.

Hydra, long a haunt of artists and, more recently, photographers, is little more than a rock with steep staircases leading up to the handsome houses once owned by seafaring families. On the tiny island of Spetses at the Gulf's southern end, fish is so delectably baked in the oven that it is worth a visit simply to taste it.

The remains of the stadium at Olympia date back to the fourth century BC. Olympia, an ancient religious sanctuary three thousand years old, is the site of the first Olympic Games in 776 BC.

An elderly woman enjoys the evening calm in front of her house on Aegina.

The red cupolas of this cruciform church on Mykonos are silhouetted against the landscape. There are about 360 churches and chapels on the island.

The Cyclades and Crete

The dazzling white villages of the Cyclades, the contours of the charming yet austere buildings gently rounded by an annual whitewash, are set in a landscape of brown rock, softened by the velvety green of the olive trees. In summer the weather is hot and dry, pleasantly cooled by the *meltemi*, a northeasterly wind. The islands are the remaining peaks of a sunken mountain range, a continuation of the eastern mainland mountains. Now numbering about 30, they include Mykonos, Delos, Tinos, Naxos, Paros and Santorini as well as lesser known islands such as Andros, Kea, Kithnos, Serifos, Milos, Ios, Sikinos and Amorgos.

Since very early times, the Cyclades have played an important role in trading between Greece and Asia Minor. Delos, the birthplace of Apollo and one of the most important shrines of antiquity, was seen by the Ancients as the centre of the encircling islands, hence the name Cyclades.

In the third and second millennia BC the Cycladic and Cretan Minoan cultures predominated in the Mediterranean.

A devastating volcanic eruption on Santorini in the 16th or 15th century BC marked the decline of the Minoan civilization. Many people believe that this region was the site of the legendary lost city of Atlantis.

The Cyclades have much in common: square houses packed around small harbours, against a backdrop of steep mountainsides; narrow streets with endless flights of steps, tiny domes and churches with twin towers or cupolas; places of pilgrimage and ancient archaeological sites; windmills and Venetian forts. The arrival of tourism in the 1970s in the form of island-hoppers with dreams of freedom and beauty in their back-packs, brought a new source of income for the previously poor islanders and halted emigration.

The island cuisine is simple and uses relatively few basic ingredients. Many dishes include minced meat: m*oussaka*, aubergine and mince bake; *pastitsio*, meat and macaroni pie; or *kolokithakia avgolemono*, stuffed courgettes with egg and lemon sauce.

Naxos, the largest of the Cyclades, with many springs, is a fertile island of orange and lemon groves, vineyards, figs, pomegranates and honey. It also produces aromatic banana and lemon liqueurs and some interesting cheeses, as do other islands such as Sifnos. The best thyme honey can be found on Kea. Paros, famous for its translucent white marble as well as its beauty, produces a full-bodied red wine, Kavarnis, good drunk with *stifado*, a meat and onion stew. The vines planted in sheltered hollows on the volcanic Santorini produce good wines now exported in quantity—dry Thira and sweet Vinsanto whites, Santino and Atlantis reds.

As elsewhere in Greece, Easter and other religious festivals—such as the Feast of the Assumption on August 15 and individual patron saints' days—are enthusiastically celebrated on all the islands, and regional costumes are worn. On March 25 and August 15, pilgrims flock to Tinos, island of 800 Venetian dovecotes, to worship at the miracle-working icon of the Virgin Mary.

Crete

Crete, 250 kilometres long by 60 kilometres wide, is the largest of the Greek islands and, because it is only 300 kilometres away from the North African coast, historically an important link between Europe, North Africa and Eastern Asia. The first settlers are thought to have arrived about 7,000 years ago. Of the splendours of the golden era of Minoan civilization 400 to 500 years later, there is still some evidence at the palace of Knossos, near Heraklion, and other important sites.

Despite Turkish and Venetian rule, and more recently the German occupation during the Second World War, the Cretans have retained their strong independent spirit, and island life is an intensely enjoyable affair. For the many visitors there are fine beaches, archaeological sites and wonderful walks through mountainous country scented with wild herbs.

The best impression of Crete's culinary delights can be gained by visiting the street market in Heraklion or market hall in Chania. Herbs are used to add a delicate flavour to ewe's cheeses. Local yogurt and honey is a special treat. Cretan bread sprinkled with olive oil is another; Crete has 24 million olive trees, 48 per inhabitant.

Over a daily glass of ouzo at the kafeneon, the men of a village discuss local gossip or world events. In rural areas the women rarely join them.

The island has produced wine for 4,500 years. The main growing area is at Archanes, near Heraklion. Among the better reds are Archanes, Daphnes, Peza and Sitia; there are also some fresh, fruity whites. The local retsina is also worth tasting, as is the strong local *raki*, or *tsikoudia*, a spirit distilled from grape skins and stalks.

A flourishing arbour of bougainvillea shades customers of this taverna near Kritsa on Crete from the midday sun. Kritsa is famous for its weaving, considered to be among the best in Crete.

The windmills on the slopes of Profitis Ilias, near the charming village of Olimbos, are one of the main sights of Karpathos. Olimbos, situated at the more isolated northern end of the island, is Karpathos' oldest village.

Rhodes, the Dodecanese and the Northeast Aegean islands

The Dodecanese, or "12 islands", were first grouped together in the time of the Crusaders and the Knights of St. John. Later, they were joined by Rhodes and Kos. After nearly 400 years of Turkish rule, they were ceded to Italy in 1912 and returned to Greece after World War II. Now the group administratively consists of about 200 islands of which only about 16 are inhabited. Apart from Rhodes, the most important are Karpathos, Tilos, Symi, Nyssiros, Kos, Kalymnos, Leros and Patmos.

Rhodes

Rhodes is the largest island of the Dodecanese. Rhodes Town is like a picture book recounting the cosmopolitan history of the island. On summer evenings, throngs of people stroll along the marble pavement of the Knights' Quarter, worn smooth and shiny by many feet, past splendid palaces and inns. A few steps farther and the scene changes. In the shadow of the Suleiman Mosque is a swarming bazaar, with souvenir stalls and shops full of all kinds of bric-a-brac. A little farther is a classical pavilion—the fish market, a relic of the Italian occupation.

Beyond the city walls, the concrete blocks of the tourist hotels alongside the turquoise blue sea provide a not altogether agreeable contrast. The narrow streets under the Acropolis on Lindos, jewel of the island, are crowded with tourists from spring to autumn. Here the choice of food is limited to hamburgers, toasted sandwiches and *souvlakia*. Genuine island cuisine is to be found in the simple, rather shabby restaurants in the backstreets near the market, or in remote corners of the island, easily reached by bus.

Fresh, dry white wines such as Ilios and smooth reds such as Chevalier de Rhodes are recognized by wine-lovers as bywords for the wines of Rhodes. The local muscat is best chilled and drunk as an aperitif.

The Dodecanese

Karpathos rises steep and rugged out of the blue of the Aegean. High above the sea stretch the sails of ancient grain mills, and every Saturday bread is made in the village bakeries. Between August 27 and 29, the feast of St. John, the women of Olimbos take their colourful traditional costumes out of the closet and put on their jewellery and glittering headdresses.

Patmos, with its monasteries and orange groves, commemorates the

Assumption on August 15 with dancing and *diples*, sweet cakes shaped like lovers' knots. Kalymnos is an island of sponge divers, who every spring set off for the fishing grounds off the coast of North Africa not to return until the autumn. Halfway between Rhodes and Kos, now a major tourist stop, lies the hilly island of Tilos, where donkey and small boat are still the most common forms of transport.

Northeast Aegean Islands

Widely scattered across the northeast Aegean are Ikaria, Samos, Chios, Lesbos and Limnos, mountainous islands with rugged coastlines and tiny harbours situated in deep inlets. They benefit from the winter rains of the mainland, making them the envy of the Cyclades. Once ports on a profitable maritime trading route with the Orient, the islands suffered when conflict between Greece and Turkey led to the diversion of commerce. Many people emigrated, or turned to agriculture.

Lesbos, home of the ancient poet Sappho, boasts an ouzo of excellent quality, distilled in the town of Plomari. The first tourist cooperative in Greece to be run entirely by women, offering accommodation in their homes to visitors and a chance to sample traditional dishes, was founded in the village of Petra. On the west of the island is a petrified forest once buried in volcanic ash.

The small villages on Chios are almost hidden amid the greenery of mastic bushes, whose pleasant-tasting resin, once considered an aphrodisiac by the Turkish rulers, has many uses— seasoning, chewing gum, liqueur, antiseptic and varnish. Limnos, from

where in 1915 the British launched their unsuccessful attack on the Dardanelles, and fertile Samos further south close to the Turkish coast, are renowned for their sweet golden muscat wines, made from grapes grown on narrow mountainside terraces.

A fisherman mends his nets on the island of Lesbos, birthplace of the poet Sappho. Lesbos is Greece's third largest island after Crete and Euboea and of great scenic beauty.

Men break into a spontaneous dance in one of Rhodes' two harbours. Mandraki harbour, linking the old town with the new, was used by the Knights of St. John to moor their boats.

STARTERS AND SALADS

O n warm summer evenings,
when friends gather in tavernas
over a glass of wine or ouzo,
the table does not stay empty for long.
Greeks rarely drink without eating,
whether it is just a bowl of salted
almonds or, more usually, a tempting
selection of hot and cold snacks. Known
as *mezedes* or *orektika,* these appetizers
and hors-d'œuvre are traditionally served
in small oval dishes and plates; brought
to the table as and when ready, they
provide a constantly varying choice of
flavours and aromas. Often one makes
one's own selection from a cold cabinet
display or by peeping in the cooking pots
in the taverna's kitchen.

In addition to simple snacks such as
chunks of feta cheese and plump shiny
olives, there are the popular Greek
specialities of stuffed vine leaves, dips
such as *tzatziki* and *taramosalata,* fried
seafood, savoury pies and salads. Some
delicacies vary according to the region
or season—for example, wild vegetable
salad or ragout of octopus. Some dishes
are perfect as a snack, others, such as
baked sweet peppers or prawns, make a
delicious light meal when served with
fresh, crusty bread.

If you are serving a selection of
mezedes at home, there is no need for
individual plates; just hand each guest a
fork and let them help themselves from
the array of serving dishes—a way of
eating especially characteristic of
Greece's little *ouzerias,* or ouzo bars.

Piperies sto fourno

Not difficult · Central Greece

Baked sweet peppers

Serves 4

500 g sweet green or red peppers
1 medium-sized onion
2 garlic cloves
300 g tomatoes
5 tbsp olive oil
2 tbsp tomato purée
15 g dill
salt
freshly ground black pepper
150 g kefalograviera or, if
unavailable, Gruyère cheese
50 g feta cheese

Preparation time: 50 minutes

990 kJ/240 calories per portion

1 Preheat the oven to 220°C (425°F or Mark 7). Wash and dry the sweet peppers. Peel and finely dice the onion and the garlic. Plunge the tomatoes briefly into boiling water and remove the skins. Dice the flesh.

2 Heat 3 tbsp of the olive oil in a frying pan over medium heat. Fry the peppers on all sides, until they begin to soften but have not browned. Remove them from the pan and set aside.

3 Add the remaining oil to the pan and sauté the onion and garlic until transparent. Stir in the diced tomato, together with any juices, and fry over high heat for 5 minutes. Dilute the tomato purée with 30 cl water and add it to the pan. Cover, and cook over medium heat for about 5 minutes.

4 Rinse the dill and shake dry. Coarsely chop the leaves and stir them into the sauce. Season with salt and pepper and transfer the mixture to a large baking dish. Lay the peppers on top of the sauce and bake in the centre of the oven for about 15 minutes.

5 Coarsely grate the *kefalograviera* cheese, and crumble the feta. Sprinkle both cheeses evenly over the peppers and bake for a further 5 minutes. Serve hot or warm with fresh, crusty bread.

Wine: Retsina or a light red *vin ordinaire* goes well with this dish.

Note: Long, narrow sweet peppers are best for this dish. If you can only find large round ones, cut them in half and deseed before cooking.

Tzatziki

Yogurt with cucumber

3 small ridged cucumbers, or 1
large firm cucumber (about 400 g)
salt
2 to 3 garlic cloves
600 g Greek yogurt (see Note,
below)
2 sprigs fresh mint
1 tbsp white wine vinegar
2 tbsp olive oil

Preparation time: 25 minutes
(plus 10 minutes' chilling time)

830 kJ/200 calories per portion

1 Wash and trim the cucumbers and coarsely grate the flesh, including the skin. Stir in 1 tsp salt, then leave to stand for about 10 minutes. Pour off any liquid that has formed, then place the grated cucumber in a sieve and gently squeeze out the remaining excess water. Peel the garlic. Wash the mint and shake dry.

2 Transfer the cucumber to a bowl and mix in the yogurt. Press the garlic into the bowl through a garlic presser, add the vinegar and olive oil, and stir well. Season with salt and refrigerate for about 10 minutes. Serve chilled, garnished with mint leaves.

Wine: A light dry white wine, such as a Côtes de Meliton from northern Greece, or a retsina, is good with *tzatziki*.

Note: Thin, low-fat yogurts may need to be strained. Use a coffee filter bag inside a conical sieve or a fine sieve lined with muslin, pour in the yogurt and stand it over a bowl for about 20 minutes. Although *tzatziki* is usually served simply as a snack or starter with bread, it is also a delicious accompaniment to grilled lamb chops or baked or grilled fish.

Gigantes plaki

Beans in tomato sauce

250 g dried haricot beans
1 bay leaf
1 medium-sized onion
2 garlic cloves
300 g tomatoes
4 tbsp olive oil
3 tbsp tomato purée
½ tsp sugar
½ tsp hot paprika
2 to 3 fennel sprigs, leaves only
salt

Preparation time: 2¼ hours
(plus 8 to 12 hours' soaking time)

1300 kJ/310 calories per portion

1 Rinse the beans under cold running water, then put them in a bowl with plenty of cold water, cover and leave to soak overnight. Drain the beans and transfer them to a large pan. Cover with fresh water, add the bay leaf and bring to the boil. Remove the scum as it forms, then cover the pan and simmer over low heat for about 45 minutes.

2 Peel and finely dice the onion and the garlic. Plunge the tomatoes briefly in boiling water, remove the skins and dice the flesh.

3 Heat the oil in another pan, and fry the onion and garlic until transparent. Dilute the tomato purée with ½ litre water, and add it to the pan together with the tomatoes, sugar and paprika.

4 Cover the pan and simmer the sauce over low heat. When the beans have cooked for 45 minutes, remove them with a slotted spoon and stir them into the tomato sauce. Rinse the fennel leaves, chop and stir into the sauce.

5 Cover the pan and simmer the beans in the sauce over low heat for a further hour, stirring from time to time. If the sauce becomes too thick, add a little boiling water as necessary. When the beans are tender, remove the bay leaf, season with salt and serve warm.

Note: For added flavour, chop up some small smoked spicy sausages and add them to the beans and sauce about 20 minutes before the end of the cooking time.

Kolokithakia keftedes

Courgette fritters

300 g firm courgettes
salt
1 medium-sized onion
4 French toasts or rusks
2 eggs
30 g flat-leaf parsley
1 sprig fresh mint or ½ tsp dried mint
50 g grated kefalotyri or, if unavailable, Emmenthal cheese
freshly ground white pepper
sunflower oil for deep frying

Preparation time: 50 minutes

320 kJ/76 calories per portion

1 Wash and trim the courgettes and grate finely, including the skin. Stir in 1 tsp salt and leave to stand for about 10 minutes. Pour off any excess liquid, then leave to drain in a sieve. Peel and finely grate the onion and add it to the courgette. Squeeze out any remaining moisture, then transfer to a bowl.

2 Remove any dark crusts from the rusks, then crush the remainder with a potato masher or in a food processor. Separate the eggs. Wash and finely chop the parsley and mint. Add the rusk crumbs, grated cheese, yolks, parsley and mint to the onion and courgettes, and thoroughly mix everything together.

3 Season the mixture with salt and pepper. Whisk the egg whites until stiff, then fold them into the mixture. Pour a generous amount of oil into a deep frying pan—or to a depth of about 6 cm in a small frying pan—and heat it until small bubbles rise from a wooden spoon handle dipped into the hot oil.

4 Scoop up a teaspoonful of the courgette mixture and, with a second teaspoon, gently prise it off into the hot oil. Repeat with the rest of the mixture and fry the fritters in batches until golden-brown. Drain them on kitchen paper and serve immediately.

Agriohortasalata

Simple • Crete **Wild vegetable salad** *Serves 4*

600 g wild salad greens (for example, young dandelion leaves, nettle tips, sorrel, young spinach, ribwort, daisies, young radish tops)
1 sprig fennel
salt
3 tbsp virgin olive oil
2 tbsp lemon juice
1 unwaxed lemon

For serving:
crumbled feta cheese

Preparation time: 30 minutes

1,000 kJ/240 calories per portion

1 Sort the greens, removing any withered leaves and hard ribs or stalks. Wash thoroughly and drain.

2 Bring a large pan of salted water to the boil. Fill a large bowl with cold water and add a few ice cubes.

3 Blanch half the greens in the boiling water for about 1 minute. Remove from the pan with a slotted spoon and plunge them briefly into the ice-cold water—to prevent further cooking—and drain. Repeat with the remaining greens.

4 Wash and chop the fennel. Arrange the greens on a serving dish, sprinkle lightly with salt and the chopped fennel, and dribble on the olive oil and lemon juice. Serve immediately, garnished with wedges of lemon and accompanied by the crumbled feta cheese and fresh wholemeal bread.

Wine: A dry white wine, such as one from Peza in Crete, is a good choice to accompany this salad.

Note: The majority of greens called for here are also available in the shops, but good substitutes include rocket, watercress, Swiss chard greens, lamb's lettuce, purslane and mustard greens.

Wild vegetables

With the first drops of autumn rain, the Greek countryside erupts into a luscious green carpet of plants and flowers. So begins the season—lasting until late spring, when the rains cease—of the much-coveted wild and cultivated greenstuffs known as *agriohorta*, or *horta*.

Many of the plants that flourish in the meadows and mountain pastures of Greece are the precursors of cultivated vegetables such as red chicory, asparagus, spinach and radish. Others are more commonly regarded as weeds—dandelions, for example. These wild delicacies are a feature of rural Greek cuisine,

adding variety to both cooked dishes and salads. Some are aromatic (fennel), some slightly bitter (young spinach), some astringent (sorrel), yet others herby or peppery (watercress, rocket).

Varieties of the above salad greens are available in supermarkets and greengrocers; when buying, look for

bright, fresh leaves and use them as soon as possible. When collecting wild hedgerow plants such as nettle tips or dandelion leaves, choose young, tender specimens and gather them before they flower. Do not pick plants from the roadside: they will have absorbed petrol fumes.

Taramosalata

Fish roe purée

Fairly easy • Northern Greece

Serves 4

2 day-old white bread rolls
(about 200 g)
100 to 125 g tarama or, if
unavailable, fresh smoked cod's roe
3 tbsp olive oil
3 to 4 tbsp lemon juice
30 g parsley
50 g black olives

Preparation time: 30 minutes
(plus 1 hour's chilling time)

940 kJ/220 calories per portion

1 Shave the crusts off the rolls and discard. Moisten the rolls by briefly soaking them in warm water, then squeeze out the excess moisture. Pull the bread apart with your fingers and, using a fork, mash it to a thin pulp. Add the *tarama*, then with your hands or a wooden spoon, work the *tarama* and the bread together to make a paste.

2 Add the olive oil and the lemon juice alternately, a little at a time, stirring with a wooden spoon to make a smooth, creamy purée. Adjust the seasoning as necessary—*taramosalata* should taste subtly fishy, rather than overpoweringly so.

3 Cover the *taramosalata* and refrigerate for about an hour. Before serving, rinse the parsley and shake dry. Arrange the leaves round the edge of a serving plate. Stir the purée once again, then spoon it onto the centre of the plate. Garnish with the olives and serve with fresh white bread or pitta.

Wine: A well-chilled retsina is the best choice to accompany *taramosalata*.

Note: *Tarama*, the salted coral-pink roe of the female grey mullet, is sold by Greek or Middle Eastern food shops. Fresh smoked cod's roe is also stocked by fishmongers and good supermarkets.

Midia tiganita

Deep-fried mussels

Needs a little care • Northern Greece

Serves 4

1 egg
1 tbsp olive oil
freshly ground white pepper • salt
100 g flour
1.5 kg fresh mussels
1 carrot • 1 medium-sized onion
1 stick celery • 1 bay leaf
1 tsp black peppercorns
2 cloves
3 cm piece unwaxed lemon rind
¼ litre dry white wine
sunflower or vegetable oil
2 lemons
parsley and rocket for garnish

Preparation time: 1¼ hours

730 kJ/170 calories per portion

1 In a bowl, whisk the egg with the olive oil, 12.5 cl water and a little pepper and salt. Stir in the flour and mix well. Cover the batter and leave it to stand for about 1 hour. Meanwhile, scrape the mussels under running cold water and remove the beards with the blunt edge of a knife. Tap any shells that are open, and discard those that do not close. Peel and slice the carrot and onion. Wash and slice the celery.

2 Place the vegetables in a large pan with the bay leaf, peppercorns, cloves, lemon rind, 1 tsp salt, the wine and ¼ litre water, and bring to the boil. Cook for a few minutes, then add the mussels and cook over medium heat for

about 5 minutes, shaking the pan from time to time, until the mussels open. Leave to cool for 30 minutes, discarding any mussels that remain closed.

3 Remove the mussels from the shells and allow to drain. Pour a generous amount of oil into a deep frying pan—or to a depth of about 6 cm in a small frying pan—and heat it until bubbles rise from a wooden spoon handle when it is dipped into the oil. Dip the mussels in the batter to coat them and fry them until golden. Drain on kitchen paper and serve immediately, garnished with lemon wedges, parsley and rocket.

Wine: A dry white wine from Santorini is excellent with mussels.

Patsaria salata

Simple • Northern Greece

Beetroot salad

Serves 4

1 kg small beetroots, with greens
4 tbsp red wine vinegar
salt
2 garlic cloves
30 g parsley
3 tbsp virgin olive oil
freshly ground black pepper

Preparation time: 1½ to 2 hours
(plus 1 hour's standing time)

730 kJ/170 calories
per portion

1 Cut off the beetroot greens 5 to 8 cm above the root and set aside. Wash the beetroots, and place them in a pan with sufficient water to cover. Bring to the boil, then simmer over low heat for 1 to 1½ hours, depending on size, until tender.

2 Drain the beetroots and rinse in cold water. Trim, peel and halve them, then cut into thickish slices and set aside. Cut the stalks and leaves into 3 cm pieces. Place in a pan, add water to cover and cook for about 15 minutes, until tender but still crisp. About 2 minutes before the end of the cooking time, stir in the vinegar and salt.

3 Remove the pan from the heat, add the sliced beetroot, stir to mix with the leaves and leave to cool. Then cover and refrigerate for about 1 hour.

4 Meanwhile, peel the garlic and chop coarsely. Wash the parsley, shake dry and chop finely. With a slotted spoon, remove the sliced beetroot, stalks and leaves from the stock. Place them in a bowl and pour over the olive oil. Add a little more vinegar to taste, sprinkle with the chopped garlic, parsley and pepper, and serve.

Horiatiki salata

Country salad

400 g medium-sized tomatoes
1 cucumber
250 g large red onions
300 g medium-sized sweet green peppers
100 g black olives, pickled in vinegar
3 tbsp wine vinegar
4 tbsp virgin olive oil
salt
freshly ground black pepper
200 g feta cheese
½ tsp dried oregano

Preparation time: 20 minutes

1,500 kJ/360 calories per portion

1 Wash the tomatoes and cucumber thoroughly. Cut each tomato into eight wedges. Trim the ends of the cucumber and cut it into thick slices; if you prefer smaller pieces, halve the slices.

2 Peel and halve the onions and cut into thickish slices. Wash and halve the sweet peppers and remove the ribs and seeds. Cut the flesh into thick strips.

3 Arrange the tomatoes, cucumber, onion, peppers and olives in a wide bowl or serving dish. Mix together the vinegar, 3 tbsp olive oil, and salt and dribble the dressing over the salad. Sprinkle with black pepper.

4 Thickly slice—or if you prefer, coarsely crumble—the cheese, and arrange it on top of the salad. Sprinkle with the oregano and the remaining olive oil and serve immediately.

Variation: For variety, you can add anchovy fillets, strips of cos lettuce, capers or sliced hard-boiled eggs. If you prefer, you can substitute lemon juice for the vinegar in the dressing.

Note: In Greece, this salad is usually placed in the middle of the table, allowing everyone to help themselves straight from the bowl.

Lachanosalata me karota

Easy • Northern Greece **Cabbage, carrot and egg salad** *Serves 4*

2 eggs
½ small white cabbage
(about 400 g)
300 g medium-sized carrots
30 g parsley
4 tbsp virgin olive oil
juice of 1 lemon
salt
few drops honey
freshly ground black pepper
100 g black olives, pickled in
vinegar

Preparation time: 30 minutes

950 kJ/230 calories per portion

1 Hard boil the eggs, then plunge them into cold water to cool. Wash and trim the cabbage, cut out and discard the hard core and the blemished outer leaves. Cut the rest lengthwise into four pieces and shred finely. Transfer to a serving dish.

2 Peel the carrots and cut them lengthwise into very thin, short strips or coarsely grate them. Heap them on top of the cabbage. Rinse the parsley and shake dry. Coarsely chop the leaves and sprinkle them over the carrots and cabbage.

3 In a small bowl, mix together the olive oil, lemon juice, salt, honey and a little black pepper. Pour the dressing over the salad.

4 Shell the eggs and cut them into quarters. Arrange the pieces of egg and the olives on top of the salad and serve.

Variation: You can substitute red cabbage for the white to make another delicious, crisp salad.

Salata fassolia mavromatica

Not difficult • Mainland Greece **Black-eyed pea salad** *Serves 4*

300 g dried black-eyed peas
1 bay leaf
3 tbsp virgin olive oil
3 to 4 tbsp wine vinegar
salt
sugar
freshly ground black pepper
200 g spring onions
300 g tomatoes
30 g parsley
3 sprigs fresh mint

Preparation time: 1¼ hours
(plus 8 to 12 hours' soaking time,
and 1 hour for cooling)

1,400 kJ/330 calories per portion

1 Rinse the peas under running water. Transfer them to a large bowl, cover with plenty of water and leave to soak overnight.

2 Drain the peas, then place them in a large pan. Add the bay leaf and enough fresh water to cover, and bring to the boil. Remove the scum as it forms and cook over low heat, covered, for 35 to 45 minutes, until the peas are tender.

3 Drain the peas and let them stand until they stop steaming, then transfer them to a bowl. Stir in the olive oil, vinegar, salt, a little sugar and a generous amount of pepper, and leave to cool for about 1 hour.

4 Meanwhile, trim, wash and slice the spring onions. Plunge the tomatoes briefly in boiling water, skin them and finely chop the flesh.

5 Rinse the parsley and mint under running water and shake dry. Finely chop half and set aside the remainder. Stir the spring onions, tomatoes and chopped herbs into the cooked peas and season with salt and pepper. Arrange on a serving dish, garnish with the remaining parsley and mint leaves, and serve.

Variation: For extra flavour, add sweet red or green pepper rings and black olives.

Dako

Quick and easy • Crete

Toasted bread with cheese, onion and tomato topping

Serves 4

One day-old rye baguette
300 g tomatoes
150 g red onions
8 tbsp virgin olive oil
salt
freshly ground black pepper
1 tbsp lemon juice
200 g feta cheese
1 tsp dried oregano

Preparation time: 35 minutes

2,000 kJ/480 calories per portion

1 Preheat the oven to 150°C (300°F or Mark 2). Cut the baguette in half lengthwise, then in half again crosswise. Place the pieces on a baking sheet in the oven, cut side up, and leave them to dry out for about 15 minutes. Remove from the oven and allow to cool. Briefly dip each of the pieces of bread in water, then let them stand to soak up the moisture.

2 Wash and halve the tomatoes and peel the onions. Finely dice the onions and the tomatoes. Arrange the pieces of bread side by side on a serving dish and sprinkle them evenly with half the olive oil.

3 Spread the diced tomato and onion on top of the bread pieces. Season with salt and pepper, then sprinkle with the lemon juice and 2 tbsp olive oil. Coarsely crumble the cheese on top, sprinkle with the oregano and the remaining olive oil, and serve.

Wine: A full-bodied red Archanes wine from Crete goes well with this dish.

Note: Many Greeks, especially in rural areas, still make their own bread at home and then take it to be baked—for a small charge—in the clay ovens of their local bakery. Bakers will often obligingly cook other dishes that are brought to them by their neighbours.

Fava

Not difficult • Northern Greece

Split-pea purée

Serves 4

300 g dried yellow split peas
1 bay leaf
1 medium-sized onion
salt
freshly ground black pepper
3 tbsp lemon juice
4 tbsp virgin olive oil
15 g parsley
1 garlic clove
1 small red sweet pepper
3 spring onions (about 150 g)

Preparation time: 1 hour 45 minutes

710 kJ/170 calories per portion

1 Rinse the split peas under cold running water, then transfer them to a large pan. Add the bay leaf and enough fresh water to cover.

2 Peel and dice the onion and add it to the peas. Bring to the boil and remove the scum from the surface. Cover, and simmer over low heat for about 1 hour, or until the peas begin to disintegrate.

3 Drain the peas through a sieve, and remove the bay leaf. With the back of a wooden spoon, purée the peas by pressing them through the sieve; alternatively, use a food processor. Stir vigorously.

4 Stir in the salt, pepper, lemon juice and 3 tbsp olive oil, adjusting the seasoning if necessary. Rinse the parsley under running water, shake dry, and chop coarsely. Peel the garlic and crush the flesh. Stir the garlic and parsley into the purée.

5 Wash, halve and deseed the pepper and cut the flesh into thin strips. Wash and trim the spring onions, and cut into pieces. Place the purée on a serving dish and sprinkle with the remaining olive oil. Garnish with the strips of pepper and spring onion, and serve.

Saganaki
Fried cheese

Serves 4

400 g kefalograviera or other firm-textured cheese (for example, kefalotyri, haloumi, Gruyère or Parmesan)
1 egg
2 tbsp flour
3 tbsp olive oil
1 unwaxed lemon

Preparation time: 20 minutes

1,300 kJ/310 calories per portion

1 Cut the cheese into 1 cm-thick slices. Break the egg onto a deep plate and whisk it with a fork. Sift the flour onto a flat plate. Turn the oven to the lowest setting and place four plates on the middle shelf to warm.

2 Heat the oil in a medium-sized frying pan. Dip the cheese slices first in the beaten egg, then in the flour, shaking off any excess flour. Fry the cheese slices in the hot oil for about 30 seconds on each side until they are a pale golden colour. Briefly drain on kitchen paper.

3 Cut the lemon into wedges. Serve the cheese slices immediately on the warm plates, garnished with the lemon wedges, so that everyone can squeeze on lemon juice to taste.

Drink: Retsina or ouzo with iced water goes well with this dish.

Variation: For an easy and filling supper, serve *saganaki* with fried eggs.

Note: This dish takes its name from the little round, black-handled frying pan in which it is traditionally cooked and taken to the table.

Garides giouvetsi
Baked prawns

Fairly easy • Thessaloniki

Serves 4

200 g spring onions
1 garlic clove
300 g tomatoes
4 tbsp olive oil
4 tbsp dry white wine
salt
freshly ground black pepper
400 g cooked, unpeeled prawns
30 g dill
100 g feta cheese

Preparation time: 50 minutes

**1,200 kJ/290 calories
per portion**

1 Preheat the oven to 225°C (425°F or Mark 7). Wash and trim the spring onions and chop them into small pieces. Peel and finely dice the garlic. Plunge the tomatoes briefly in boiling water and skin. Dice the flesh.

2 Heat the oil in a pan. Fry the onions and garlic until transparent. Stir in the diced tomato and wine, and cook over medium heat for about 5 minutes, if necessary, adding up to 5 tbsp hot water. Season with salt and pepper.

3 Wash the prawns under running water and drain. Shell them, leaving the tails on, but removing the heads and dark, vein-like intestines. Wash the dill

under running water, shake dry and chop coarsely. Stir the prawns and chopped dill into the tomato sauce.

4 Transfer the prawn mixture to an ovenproof dish. Crumble the feta cheese and sprinkle it over the prawns. Bake in the centre of the oven for 10 minutes, or until lightly browned. Serve with freshly baked bread.

Variation: Substitute 300 g spinach for the tomato. Wash, derib and coarsely chop the spinach, and add it to the onions and garlic together with the wine. Cook over medium heat for about 15 minutes, and proceed as above.

Kalamarakia tiganita

Fairly easy • Ionian islands **Deep-fried baby squid**   *Serves 4*

600 g cleaned baby squid or
baby cuttlefish
2 eggs
2 tbsp flour
sunflower oil
salt
2 unwaxed lemons

Preparation time: 45 minutes

670 kJ/160 calories per portion

1 Wash the squid under cold water, rinsing out the pouches well. Separate the tentacles from the rest of the body. Pat dry with kitchen paper.

2 Whisk the eggs in a deep plate. Sift the flour onto a flat plate. Pour a generous amount of oil into a deep frying pan—or to a depth of about 6 cm in a small frying pan—and heat the oil until bubbles rise from a wooden spoon handle when it is dipped into the oil.

3 Lightly sprinkle the squid pieces with salt. Dip them first in the beaten egg then in the flour and fry until pale golden. Drain on kitchen paper.

4 Cut the lemons into quarters. Serve the fried squid immediately, accompanied by the lemon wedges.

Wine: A dry white wine from the Peloponnese is excellent with this dish.

Note: For a light but satisfying meal, serve the squid with a simple salad and potato and garlic purée (*see below*).

Skordalia me patates

Simple • Ionian islands **Garlic and potato purée**   *Serves 4*

400 g waxy potatoes
3 garlic cloves
5 tbsp virgin olive oil
6 to 7 tbsp chicken stock
juice of 1 lemon
salt
cos lettuce heart
50 g black olives

Preparation time: 1 hour

890 kJ/210 calories per portion

1 Wash the potatoes, cover with water and cook for 30 to 35 minutes. Drain, rinse briefly in cold water, then peel them while they are still hot. With the back of a wooden spoon, purée the potatoes by pressing them through a fine sieve into a bowl.

2 Peel the garlic cloves, pound them with a mortar and pestle, or crush them through a garlic presser, and stir into the potato. Add the olive oil, chicken stock, lemon juice and a little salt, adjusting the seasoning if necessary. For a more piquant flavour, add slightly more olive oil and salt, and stir again thoroughly.

3 Separate the lettuce leaves, wash carefully, shake dry, and arrange on a flat serving dish. Spoon the potato and garlic purée in the centre. Rinse the olives under cold running water and use them to garnish the purée.

Variation: For a more delicate flavour, stir 2 tbsp grated, peeled almonds and 2 to 3 more tbsp of chicken stock into the purée .

Note: Garlic and potato purée makes an ideal light starter to a meal, or an accompaniment to grilled meat or fish, or deep-fried squid (*see above*).

Dolmades
Stuffed vine leaves

300 g fresh or preserved vine leaves
200 g long grain rice
200 g medium-sized onions
5 tbsp olive oil
4 tbsp pine-nuts
4 tbsp currants
salt
sugar
freshly ground black pepper
allspice
15 g parsley
15 g dill
2 sprigs fresh mint
juice of 1 lemon
1 unwaxed lemon
fresh vine leaves for garnish
(optional)

Preparation time: 2½ hours
(plus 1 hour's cooling time)

1,100 kJ/260 calories per portion

1 Bring a large pan of water to the boil. If using fresh vine leaves, wash them, then immerse briefly in the boiling water—leave a little longer if the leaves are older. If using preserved leaves, carefully separate, rinse, then immerse them in the water for 5 to 8 minutes. Remove with a slotted spoon, drain well, and lay them out on a cloth.

2 Rinse the rice and drain well. Peel the onions and grate into a small bowl. Heat 3 tbsp of the oil in a pan, and briefly fry the pine-nuts and currants. Stir in the rice and onions and fry over medium heat until transparent. Add 40 cl water, salt, and a little sugar, pepper and allspice. Cover and cook over low heat for about 15 minutes, occasionally stirring, until the rice is almost cooked.

3 Meanwhile, rinse the parsley, dill and mint under running water and shake dry. Finely chop all three and stir them into the rice. Lay the vine leaves on a work surface and, if necessary, cut off the thick stems. Place 1 tsp of the rice stuffing at the base of each leaf (*above*).

4 Fold the bottom edge of the leaf over the filling, followed by the left and right edges, one on top of the other (*above*).

5 Continue rolling the whole leaf up towards the tip to make a small sausage-shaped package (*above*). To prevent them from sticking, line the base of a wide-based pan with 3 to 4 vine leaves. Arrange the stuffed leaves close together in layers, with the leaf-ends downwards. Pour over the lemon juice and the remaining olive oil.

6 Weight down the stuffed leaves with an inverted plate, add enough hot water to cover the plate and simmer over low heat for about 1 hour, or until all the liquid is absorbed. Remove from the heat and leave to cool for about 1 hour. Serve, if you like, on a bed of fresh vine leaves, garnished with slices of lemon.

Wine: A fruity rosé from Rhodes is an ideal choice to accompany this classic Greek dish.

SOUPS

S oups are one of the mainstays of Greek cuisine, particularly in rural areas, where they are seen as providing a healthy and hearty alternative to meat, never widely available or relied upon in Greece. Pulse-based soups are a cheap, easily prepared source of fibre and protein, and are especially valued in the harsh winters, and throughout Lent, when a diet free from meat and other animal products is encouraged. There are also popular light soups, such as the refreshing chicken soup with egg and lemon, or *kotosoupa avgolemono*.

One of the most famous Greek soups is *mayiritsa*, made from the head, heart, liver and lungs of the Paschal lamb. It is traditionally served just once a year, after the midnight service on Easter Saturday; the milk-fed lamb being roasted whole the following day.

Another offal-based soup is *patsas*, a warming and nourishing dish often served by tavernas for breakfast to workers on the early shift, or home-bound late-night revellers. Also a favourite is the fish soup *kakavia*, the recipe for which is said to have been taken to southern France by colonizing Greek settlers and to have inspired the famous Marseilles *bouillabaisse*.

In Greece, soup is always served with plenty of fresh bread. For an easy, filling meal, simply present one of these soups with bread, a seasonal vegetable or green salad, and a few olives.

Soupa fakes

Not difficult • Northern Greece **Lentil soup**

Serves 4

250 g green lentils
1 medium-sized onion
2 garlic cloves
200 g carrots
1 stick celery
300 g tomatoes
4 tbsp olive oil
1 tbsp tomato purée
2 bay leaves • 1 sprig fresh thyme
salt • freshly ground black pepper
30 g parsley
red wine vinegar
100 g green or black olives

Preparation time: 1¼ hours

1,700 kJ/400 calories per portion

1 Rinse the lentils in a sieve under cold running water and drain. Peel and finely dice the onion and the garlic. Peel the carrots, halve lengthwise, then slice thinly. Wash the celery, dice the stalk and coarsely chop the leaves. Plunge the tomatoes briefly in boiling water, skin and dice the flesh.

2 Heat the oil in a large saucepan over medium heat. Sauté the onion, garlic, carrots, celery, tomatoes and tomato purée for about 2 minutes, stirring constantly. Add 1.5 litres water, the lentils, bay leaves and thyme, and bring to the boil.

3 Reduce the heat to low, cover the pan and simmer the soup for 30 to 40 minutes, or until the lentils are soft. Season with salt and pepper. Rinse and dry the parsley, chop coarsely and stir into the soup. Serve accompanied by a little jug of vinegar and a bowl of olives. Season the soup to taste at the table with 1 to 2 tsp vinegar and a few olives.

Variation:
Lentil soup with spinach
Instead of the tomatoes, stir 500 g washed, trimmed and coarsely chopped spinach into the soup about 10 minutes before the end of the cooking time.

Kotosoupa avgolemono

Needs a little care • Mainland Greece **Chicken soup with egg and lemon**

Serves 4

1 ready-cleaned boiling fowl (about 1.2 kg)
salt
1 bay leaf
200 g carrots
1 onion
1 thin leek
1 stick celery
60 g long-grain rice
freshly ground black pepper
2 eggs
juice of 1 lemon
15 g parsley

Preparation time: 2 hours

2,100 kJ/500 calories per portion (including sauce)

1 Rinse the chicken under running water and place in a large pan. Add salt, the bay leaf and 1.5 litres cold water, and bring to the boil. Skim off the scum, reduce the heat to low, cover the pan and simmer for about 1 hour.

2 Peel and dice the carrots and the onion. Trim the leek, cutting off the dark green leaves, and cut in half lengthwise. Wash, then slice thinly. Trim and wash the celery, slice the stalk and coarsely chop the leaves. Rinse the rice under running water.

3 Remove the bird from the stock and set aside to cool. Skim the fat from the stock, strain it and return to the pan. Add the chopped vegetables and rice,

and simmer for about 25 minutes. Remove the meat from the bird, cut it into bite-sized pieces and add to the soup. If the soup needs thinning, add a little water. Leave to cool slightly.

4 Season the soup with salt and pepper. Thoroughly whisk the eggs and lemon juice in a bowl, then whisk them into the soup. Gently reheat the soup, but do not let it boil otherwise it will curdle. Rinse the parsley, coarsely chop the leaves and sprinkle them over the soup before serving.

Note: Avgolemono sauce, based on eggs and lemon, is used throughout Greek cuisine, in soups and stews as well as with fish, poultry and vegetables.

Revithia soupa
Chick-pea soup

Takes a little time • Most regions

Serves 4

250 g dried chick-peas
1 large onion
1 medium-sized carrot
5 tbsp olive oil
salt
freshly ground black pepper
30 g parsley
1 unwaxed lemon

**Preparation time: 1¾ hours
(plus 12 hours' soaking time)**

1,400 kJ/330 calories per portion

1 Rinse the chick-peas under running water. Transfer them to a large bowl, cover with plenty of fresh water and leave them to soak overnight.

2 Drain the chick-peas, place them in a pan with 1.5 litres cold water, and bring to the boil. Skim off the scum as it forms, cover the pan and cook over low heat for about 1 hour.

3 Meanwhile, peel the onion and the carrot and cut into small dice. After 1 hour, stir the onion, carrot and olive oil into the soup, and continue to cook for a further 30 minutes until the vegetables and chick-peas are tender.

4 Season the soup with salt and pepper. Rinse the parsley under running water, chop the leaves and stir into the soup. Wash the lemon and cut it into wedges. Serve the soup with a dish of lemon wedges, so that lemon juice can be added to taste at the table.

Note: Many Greek cooks like to make a more refined soup by skinning the chick-peas after soaking. However, as well as being time-consuming, this means the loss of the valuable fibre contained in the skins.

Soupa horiatiki
Peasant soup

Not difficult · Central Greece

180 g medium-sized onions
2 thin leeks
300 g carrots
3 sticks celery
150 g rindless streaky bacon
300 g small courgettes
200 g tomatoes
200 g medium-sized waxy potatoes
6 tbsp olive oil
salt
30 g parsley
freshly ground black pepper
1 tsp dried oregano

Preparation time: 1¼ hours

2,000 kJ/480 calories per portion

1 Peel and finely dice the onions. Trim the leeks, cut them in half lengthwise, and wash well. Slice thinly. Peel and dice the carrots. Wash the celery and slice thinly. Dice the bacon.

2 Wash the courgettes, top and tail them and cut into slices about 1 cm thick. Plunge the tomatoes briefly into boiling water, skin them and dice the flesh. Peel and dice the potatoes.

3 Heat half the olive oil in a large saucepan over medium heat and fry the bacon for about 1 minute. Stir in the onions, leeks, carrots, celery and potatoes and continue cooking for a further minute. Stir in 1.25 litres hot water and a little salt. Bring to the boil, then reduce the heat to low, cover the pot and cook for about 15 minutes.

4 Stir in the courgettes, tomatoes and the remaining olive oil and cook the soup for a further 15 minutes. Rinse the parsley under running water, shake dry and chop the leaves. Season the soup with salt and pepper, stir in the parsley and the oregano, and serve.

Variation: For a thicker soup, add a handful of *kritharaki*, or orzo (rice-shaped pasta), to the pan with the hot water.

Kakavia

Fish soup

Not difficult • Corfu

Serves 4

1.5 kg cleaned mixed fish or fish
fillets (for example, cod, whiting,
sea bream, mackerel, turbot)
juice of 1½ lemons
200 g onions
1 garlic clove
300 g waxy potatoes
200 g carrots
300 g tomatoes
30 g parsley
30 g celery leaves
1 bay leaf
salt
freshly ground black pepper
4 tbsp olive oil

Preparation time: 1½ hours

2,000 kJ/480 calories per portion

1 Rinse the fish under running water, then cut into large slices or pieces, put in a bowl and sprinkle with 2 to 3 tbsp of the lemon juice. Leave in a cool place.

2 Meanwhile, peel the onions, garlic, potatoes and carrots, and cut into bite-sized pieces. Plunge the tomatoes briefly into boiling water, skin and dice the flesh. Wash and finely chop the parsley and celery leaves.

3 Layer the vegetables, parsley and celery leaves in a large saucepan, add the bay leaf, and season with salt and pepper. Pour over the oil and add about 1 litre water. Bring to the boil, then reduce the heat to low and cook, covered, for about 30 minutes.

4 Add the fish pieces to the vegetables and continue to cook over low heat for a further 15 minutes. If necessary, add up to ¼ litre hot water, stirring gently.

5 With a slotted spoon, remove the fish and vegetables from the pan and arrange them on a heated serving dish. Strain the stock through a sieve, season with salt, pepper and plenty of lemon juice, and serve it separately in individual soup bowls.

Wine: A good dry white wine, such as an Ilios from the island of Rhodes, is the ideal accompaniment for this soup.

Note: If you like, chop some fresh mint and sprinkle on the fish before serving.

Soupa trahana

Trahana soup

Simple • Thrace

Serves 4

1 large onion
200 g tomatoes
130 g butter
1 litre meat stock
½ tsp dried thyme
150 g trahana (see Note, right)
30 g parsley
salt
freshly ground black pepper
100 g grated kefalotyri or
Emmenthal cheese

Preparation time: 45 minutes

1,900 kJ/450 calories per portion

1 Peel the onion and chop into small dice. Plunge the tomatoes briefly into boiling water and skin them, then dice the flesh. Heat the butter in a pan and fry the onion until transparent.

2 Stir in the tomatoes and briefly fry them with the onion. Add the meat stock and the thyme, and bring to the boil. Sprinkle in the *trahana*. Cover the pan and cook over low heat for about 20 minutes, stirring occasionally, until the soup thickens.

3 Rinse the parsley under running water, shake dry and finely chop the leaves. Season the soup with salt and pepper, and stir in the parsley. Serve, accompanied by a bowl of the grated cheese from which guests can help themselves.

Note: *Trahana* is cooked, dried and crushed wheat, sometimes blended with dried yogurt. It can be bought in specialist Greek shops.

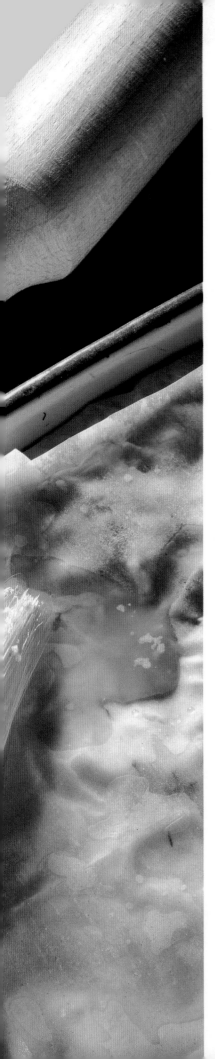

PIES

Greeks are justly proud of their pies, which are a much-loved national tradition. Routinely prepared in the home, they are also widely available from street vendors, in snack bars and in bakeries. Early in the morning, in villages across Greece, delicious smells herald the arrival of that day's batch of pies and pasties from the baker's oven.

One of the essential ingredients of these pies is wafer-thin phyllo or *yufka* pastry (*see page 59*), which is wrapped in rich buttery layers round meat, cheese or vegetable fillings. Meat pies are reserved for special occasions, but vegetable pies are eaten all year round, their stuffing varying according to the season. Fresh greens such as spinach and Swiss chard are particular favourites, although leeks, courgettes and artichokes are also widely used. Mixed just with crumbled feta cheese and fresh herbs, and encased in pastry, they make a wonderful starter or vegetarian main course. Even the humblest of ingredients, such as rice and cheese—once the only things available during harsh winters—make a delicious, yet simple meal.

These pies can be enjoyed at any time of the day. Serve them as a light snack, or, for a more filling meal, preceded by soup. In Greece, leftovers are a popular breakfast dish. Pies are also ideal picnic fare: easy to make in advance, they taste equally good cold.

Spanakopitta

Spinach pie

1 kg leaf spinach
200 g spring onions
4 tbsp olive oil
60 g dill
200 g feta cheese
salt
freshly ground black pepper
2 eggs
12.5 cl milk
80 g butter
5 large sheets phyllo pastry (see page 59)

Preparation time: about 1¾ hours

2,700 kJ/640 calories per portion

1 Wash the spinach thoroughly and remove the stalks and any hard ribs. Wash and trim the spring onions. Cut the spring onions lengthwise into four, then chop into small pieces.

2 Heat 3 tbsp olive oil in a frying pan, and fry the spring onions until transparent. Add the slightly damp spinach and continue cooking over high heat until the leaves wilt and all the liquid has evaporated. Remove the pan from the heat and allow to cool slightly. Transfer to a chopping board, chop finely and place in a bowl.

3 Chop the dill. Finely crumble the feta cheese. Mix the dill and cheese with the spinach and onion. Season with salt and pepper. Whisk the eggs and fold them into the mixture.

4 Preheat the oven to 200°C (400°F or Mark 6). Brush a round, 28 to 30 cm ovenproof flan dish with the remaining oil. Heat the milk and butter in a small pan. Unwrap the phyllo, lay the sheets on a work surface and cover with a damp cloth; remove one at a time and keep the rest covered while you work.

5 Line the flan dish with a phyllo sheet, letting the edges hang over the side. Brush it with some of the butter and milk mixture (*above*).

6 Cut the second and third sheets in half. Lay the halves in the dish, in alternating directions, brushing each with the butter and milk; let the ends hang over the side. Spoon in the spinach mixture, and press down firmly.

7 Halve the remaining two sheets, and lay the halves over the filling, again brushing each layer with butter and milk. Butter the overhanging edges and fold them over onto the pie (*above*).

8 Score the top layers of pastry to divide the pie into squares (*above*). Bake in the centre of the oven for 35 to 40 minutes, or until golden. Allow to cool slightly, then cut the pie through to the base, and serve warm or cold.

Note: This pie can also be made using the thicker *yufka* dough (*see page 59*), using half the number of sheets and brushing each layer with a generous amount of butter and milk.

Kreatopitta

Needs a little care • Epirus **Meat pie**

Serves 6 to 8

300 g medium-sized onions
30 g parsley
3 tbsp olive oil
400 g minced lamb
400 g minced beef
salt
freshly ground black pepper
1 tsp ground cinnamon
juice of 1 lemon
2 eggs
2 tbsp fresh breadcrumbs
100 g grated kefalotyri or
Emmenthal cheese
100 g feta cheese
110 g butter
1 packet phyllo pastry (about 450 g)

Preparation time: 1½ hours

2,200 kJ/520 calories per portion

1 Peel and dice the onions. Rinse the parsley under running water, shake dry and chop finely. Preheat the oven to 200°C (400°F or Mark 6).

2 Heat the oil in a frying pan and fry the onions until transparent. Add the minced lamb and beef, breaking them up with a wooden spoon, and fry over medium heat until the juices evaporate. Stir in salt, plenty of pepper, the cinnamon and the lemon juice. Remove from the heat and cool slightly.

3 Stir the eggs, breadcrumbs, grated cheese and chopped parsley into the meat mixture. Mash the feta cheese with a fork and mix it in also.

4 Melt the butter in a pan. Butter a large baking dish. Open out the phyllo sheets and cover them with a damp cloth, removing the sheets as you need them. Layer half the sheets in the dish, brushing each one with the butter. Let the edges hang over the side.

5 Check the meat for seasoning and adjust if necessary. Spoon it onto the phyllo in the dish, and press down firmly. Fold the overhanging edges up over the meat and brush with butter. Brush each of the remaining sheets with butter and layer them on top of the pie. Trim any overhang, bearing in mind that phyllo pastry shrinks as it cooks. Sprinkle a little water over the top.

6 With a sharp knife, score through the top layers of dough to make sections about 7 cm square. Bake in the centre of the oven for 45 to 50 minutes until golden. Serve warm.

Phyllo

The crisp, golden, paper-thin puff pastry known as phyllo is one of the glories of Greek and Middle Eastern cuisine. Pliable and versatile, it can be layered, folded, twisted or pleated into delicious and decorative containers for both sweet and savoury fillings, from hearty pies to delicate pastries.

Phyllo—pronounced *fee-low*—is made from flour, salt and water, kneaded to a stiff paste. This dough is divided into small pieces, covered with a damp cloth, and left to stand for 2 to 3 hours. The dough is then rolled out on a large, round board or roomy work surface with a long, thin rolling pin about 1.5 cm in diameter. Experienced cooks wield it with great dexterity, but it takes years of practice to roll out the dough to the requisite papery thinness. For this reason, most Greeks buy their phyllo ready-made from the local baker.

Phyllo is available fresh or frozen in supermarkets or specialist Greek and Middle Eastern shops. There is also a thicker Turkish version called *yufka*, suitable for more substantial pies. Frozen phyllo—which should be thawed, still wrapped, in the refrigerator—dries out easily and becomes very brittle; always keep sheets that are waiting to be used covered with a damp cloth. Thawed phyllo will keep for about a week in the refrigerator; do not refreeze it.

Mitzithropittakia

Not difficult · Crete

Cream cheese pasties

225 g flour
salt
4 tbsp olive oil
150 g mitzithra cheese or ricotta
4 spring onions (about 180 g)
2 sprigs fresh, or 1 tsp dried, mint
15 g parsley
1 egg
freshly ground black pepper

Preparation time: 1¾ hours
(including standing time)

1,200 kJ/290 calories per pasty

1 Sift the flour into a large bowl. Stir in ½ tsp salt. Make a well in the middle of the flour and pour in 1 tbsp olive oil and 10 cl water. Knead to a smooth dough. Shape the dough into a ball, wrap tightly in kitchen foil and leave to stand for about 1 hour.

2 Meanwhile, strain off any excess fluid from the cheese, and place the cheese in a small bowl. Wash and trim the spring onions. Cut them in half lengthwise, then cut into thin slices. Rinse the mint and parsley under running water, shake dry and finely chop the leaves.

3 Separate the egg and set the white aside in a small bowl. Add the yolk, spring onion and a little salt and pepper to the cheese and stir well.

4 Lightly whisk the egg white. Divide the dough in two, re-cover one half in foil and set aside. On a floured work surface, roll out the dough very thinly. Cut out circles of dough with a 12 cm diameter pastry cutter or round-rimmed glass bowl. Using half the filling, put a spoonful in the centre of each circle, and brush the edges with a little beaten egg white.

5 Fold the dough in half over the stuffing, and press the edges firmly together with the prongs of a fork (*above*). Repeat the process with the remaining dough and filling.

6 Heat the remaining olive oil in a frying pan over medium heat. Fry the pasties on both sides until golden-brown. Drain on kitchen paper, and serve warm.

Wine: A dry, fruity white wine from the Peza region of Crete goes well with these pasties.

Note: Mitzithra is a type of cottage cheese. It is sold salted for savoury fillings and unsalted for use in sweet pastries. If unavailable, ricotta makes a good alternative.

Pittes kritis

Not difficult • Crete **Little Cretan pies** **Makes about 10 pies**

400 g Swiss chard
400 g leaf spinach
4 sprigs fennel
1 thin leek
3 tbsp olive oil
100 g feta cheese
freshly ground black pepper
1 packet frozen puff pastry (about 350 g), thawed
1 egg
50 g light sesame seeds

Preparation time: 1¼ hours

2,200 kJ/520 calories per pie

1 Wash the Swiss chard and spinach and remove the stalks and hard ribs. Cut the leaves into thin strips. Rinse the fennel and chop finely. Trim the leek, remove the coarse outer leaves, cut it in half lengthwise and rinse well under running water. Slice thinly.

2 Heat the oil in a frying pan over high heat and fry the vegetables until they wilt and the fluid has evaporated. Remove the pan from the heat. Mash the cheese with a fork and add it to the vegetables. Season with pepper.

3 Preheat the oven to 225°C (425°F or Mark 7). Rinse a large baking sheet under cold running water. On a floured work surface, roll half the dough out thinly. Cut out circles with a 12 cm diameter pastry cutter or round-rimmed glass bowl. Repeat with the remaining dough. Divide the filling between the circles, putting about a spoonful in the centre of each.

4 Whisk the egg in a shallow bowl. Brush the uppermost edges of the circles with egg and fold in half. Press the edges together firmly, scoring the semi-circles with a knife for a neater look. Arrange the pies on the baking sheet, brush with egg and sprinkle with sesame seeds. Bake in the centre of the oven for 15 to 20 minutes, until golden-brown. Serve warm.

Kolokithobouriko

Not difficult • Crete **Courgette pie** **Serves 6**

800 g courgettes
3 tbsp flour
2 sheets yufka pastry (see page 59)
8 tbsp olive oil
200 g feta cheese
freshly ground black pepper
30 g dill
2 eggs
2 tbsp light sesame seeds

Preparation time: 1¾ hours

1,500 kJ/360 calories per portion

1 Wash and trim the courgettes. Cut into 5 mm thick slices. Put the flour on a plate and dip the courgette slices in flour to coat them. Open out the yufka sheets and cut them in half. Sprinkle both sides with water, cover with a damp cloth and leave to stand briefly.

2 Grease a 28 cm diameter springform cake tin with 2 tbsp oil. Lay a half sheet of dough in the tin, then another half across it, letting the edges hang over the side. Place half the courgette slices on top, overlapping one another.

3 Preheat the oven to 180°C (350°F or Mark 4). Break up the feta cheese with a fork, and spread it over the courgettes. Sprinkle with pepper. Chop the dill leaves and sprinkle them on top of the cheese. Arrange the remaining courgettes in a layer on top.

4 Lay the remaining sheets of dough across each other on the courgettes. Fold the overhanging dough edges in towards the centre, and press down. Score the upper layers of dough into 5 cm squares. Beat the eggs together with 4 tbsp water and the remaining oil and pour over the pie. Sprinkle with sesame seeds. Bake in the centre of the oven for about 1¼ hours. Serve hot.

Note: If yufka is unavailable you can use 4 sheets of phyllo instead.

Tiropittakia
Cheese triangles

½ **packet phyllo pastry (about 225 g)**
80 g butter

For the filling:
20 g butter
1 tbsp flour
4 tbsp milk
100 g cream
150 g feta cheese
50 g grated kefalograviera or
Gruyère cheese
15 g dill
30 g parsley
freshly ground black pepper
grated nutmeg

Preparation time: about 1 hour

260 kJ/62 calories per triangle

1 To make the filling, heat 20 g butter in a small pan. Add the flour and whisk to make a roux. Slowly stir in the milk and cream, and continue cooking and stirring until the sauce is smooth and thickened. Remove the pan from the heat.

2 Open out the phyllo sheets and cover them with a damp cloth. Butter a large baking sheet. Preheat the oven to 200°C (400°F or Mark 6).

3 Finely crumble the feta cheese with a fork. Stir the feta and the grated *graviera* into the white sauce. Rinse the dill and parsley under running water. Chop the leaves finely and add them to the sauce. Season with pepper and a little grated nutmeg.

4 Heat the butter in a pan. Lay two sheets of phyllo, one on top of the other, leaving the rest under the damp cloth. Cut the paired sheets into 7 by 20 cm strips. Brush the strips with melted butter. Place 1 tsp of the cheese filling about 2 cm in from the end of each strip, and fold over and over (about 5 times), zigzag fashion, to form a little triangular parcel (*above*).

5 Repeat with the remaining phyllo sheets and filling. Arrange the parcels on the baking sheet and brush with melted butter. Bake in the centre of the oven for 10 to 15 minutes until golden-brown. Serve warm.

Wine: A medium-dry Agioritikos rosé from Mount Athos in northern Greece goes well with this dish.

Note: Feta is the best known of the Greek cheeses. Traditionally made from ewe's milk—but now more usually made from cow's milk—and matured in brine, its soft crumbly texture and sharp, salty flavour has become popular far beyond Greece itself. However, *kefalograviera* (or *graviera*) is just as important in Greek cuisine. Made from ewe's or goat's milk, its consistency varies from semi-hard to hard, depending on its maturity. Its strong flavour makes it an ideal addition to savoury pies.

EGGS, PASTA AND RICE

Eggs, pasta and rice play an important role in everyday Greek cookery. Combined with vegetables and herbs—often picked wild in gardens and hedgerows—or a little meat or spicy sausage, they provide the basis of many varied and inexpensive meals. While the methods of preparation are often very simple, the results are exquisite. In rural areas or in island villages, a hungry visitor may well be welcomed with a humble, impromptu meal comprising nothing more than a wild vegetable omelette, home-baked bread and a modest country wine—and will nonetheless leave completely satisfied.

Favourite fillers are oven-baked pasta dishes such as *pastitsio,* a delicious meat and macaroni pie, or the lamb stew *giouvetsi,* whose characteristic ingredient is the rice-shaped pasta *kritharaki.* Fresh pasta, such as the small, square-shaped *hylopittes,* is popular in Greece, and is frequently home-made. Rice is enjoyed either as a side dish, or mixed with vegetables: particularly popular is rice and spinach, cooked simply with olive oil and dill and seasoned with lemon juice. Served with a topping of crumbled feta cheese, it makes a light but satisfying meal.

Omeletta agriohorta

Wild vegetable omelette

**500 g wild greens (for example,
young dandelion leaves, nettle tips,
young radish tops, sorrel, ribwort,
young spinach, watercress, daisies)
salt
4 eggs
4 tbsp olive oil
freshly ground black pepper**

**For serving:
crumbled feta cheese**

Preparation time: 25 minutes

**1,100 kJ/260 calories per portion
(if serving 4)**

1 Sort the greens, removing any hard ribs and stalks. Wash thoroughly and drain. Bring a large pan of salted water to the boil and blanch the greens in the boiling water for about 1 minute. Drain thoroughly.

2 Break the eggs into a bowl. Add 5 tbsp water and a little salt and whisk vigorously. Heat the olive oil in a medium-sized frying pan and pour in the beaten egg. Spread the vegetables on top and press them flat.

3 Cook the omelette over medium heat for 1 to 2 minutes, until it begins to set. Gently turn the omelette over and cook for a further 1 to 2 minutes. Sprinkle with pepper, and serve with white bread and a bowl of crumbled feta cheese to sprinkle over the top.

Wine: Choose a white wine from Attica, a well-chilled Rhoditis or a retsina.

Note: In Greece, omelettes are generally brought to the table whole and guests serve themselves.

Spetsofai

Eggs on a bed of vegetables

Simple • Pelion villages

Serves 4

500 g sweet green or red peppers
500 g ripe tomatoes
1 onion
2 garlic cloves
1 stick celery
15 g parsley
250 g small, smoked spicy sausages
4 tbsp olive oil
salt
freshly ground black pepper
4 eggs

Preparation time: 40 minutes

1,900 kJ/450 calories per portion

1 Wash the sweet peppers. Remove the ribs and seeds and cut the flesh lengthwise into wide strips. Plunge the tomatoes briefly into boiling water and skin. Dice the flesh.

2 Peel the onion and the garlic, and slice thinly. Wash and trim the celery and cut into pieces. Rinse the parsley under running water, shake dry and chop finely. Thickly slice the sausages.

3 Heat the olive oil in a large frying pan. Fry the sliced peppers over medium heat until browned all over. Remove from the oil with a slotted spoon and reserve.

4 Add the onion, garlic, tomatoes and celery to the pan and sauté for about 3 minutes. Mix the strips of pepper with the vegetables and keep warm.

5 In another pan, without fat, brown the slices of sausage, then mix them with the vegetables, reserving the sausage fat. Season the vegetables with salt and pepper, and stir in the parsley.

6 Fry the eggs in the fat from the sausages. Arrange them on top of the vegetables and sausages, and serve straight from the pan or on individual warmed plates, accompanied by fresh, crusty white bread.

Wine: A retsina from Attica goes well with this dish.

Note: For a more substantial main meal, serve 2 fried eggs per person.

Avga matia melitzanes

Fairly easy • Central Greece

Aubergines baked with eggs

Serves 4

**4 medium-sized aubergines (about
1 kg)
6 tbsp olive oil
4 shallots or 2 small spring onions
400 g tomatoes
30 g parsley
1 sprig fresh, or ½ tsp dried, thyme
salt
½ tsp sugar
freshly ground black pepper
8 eggs**

Preparation time: 1 hour

1,200 kJ/290 calories per portion

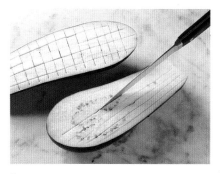

1 Wash and dry the aubergines and remove the stalks. Cut them in half lengthwise and make crisscross incisions in the flesh (*above*).

2 Heat 2 tbsp olive oil in a large non-stick frying pan. Lay four aubergine halves cut side downwards in the pan and fry them over medium heat for about 10 minutes, turning twice. Remove from the pan. Add another 2 tbsp oil and fry the remaining halves.

3 Preheat the oven to 200°C (400°F or Mark 6). Oil a large ovenproof dish. Trim the shallots or spring onions and slice thinly. Halve the tomatoes and dice the flesh. Rinse the parsley and, if using, the fresh thyme, under running water. Shake dry and chop finely.

4 Arrange the aubergines in the baking dish, cut side upwards. Scoop out the

flesh (*above*) to make room for the stuffing and the egg, and set it aside.

5 Heat the remaining olive oil in a frying pan. Sauté the onions, tomatoes and aubergine flesh over medium heat for about 5 minutes. Season with salt, sugar and pepper. Stir in the thyme and half the parsley.

6 Divide the stuffing among the aubergines halves. Make a small well

in the centre of the stuffing and break an egg into each one (*above*). Bake in the centre of the oven for 10 to 15 minutes. Sprinkle with the remaining parsley and serve immediately.

Variation: Halve the aubergines lengthwise, as above, or cut them into 1 cm-thick slices. Fry in oil over medium heat, then drain on kitchen paper. Divide into four portions. In the same pan, fry 4 slices of cooked ham until brown, then lay one slice on top of each portion of aubergine. Prepare the remaining ingredients—4 shallots (or 2 spring onions), 400 g tomatoes, 30 g parsley and 1 to 2 tsp dried thyme— as described above. Sauté them in the fat remaining in the pan, season with salt and pepper, and arrange on top of the ham. Fry the eggs with 1 tbsp oil and place one on top of each portion. Serve immediately.

Pastitsio

Meat and macaroni pie

A little more complex • Cyclades

Serves 4 to 6

500 g macaroni
salt
1 large onion • 4 tbsp olive oil
600 g minced beef
700 g tomatoes
¼ litre dry white wine
ground cinnamon • paprika
40 g butter
4 tbsp flour • ¾ litre milk
freshly ground black pepper
grated nutmeg
1 tbsp lemon juice
3 eggs
200 g grated kefalotyri cheese
30 g parsley

Preparation time: 2 hours

3,400 kJ/810 calories per portion

1 Bring a large pan of salted water to the boil and cook the macaroni until it is *al dente*. Drain. Peel and dice the onion. Heat the oil in a large frying pan over medium heat and fry the onion until transparent. Add the minced meat, and fry until well browned.

2 Preheat the oven to 180°C (350°F or Mark 4). Plunge the tomatoes briefly into boiling water and skin. Dice the flesh and add it to the meat. Stir in the wine, a little cinnamon, paprika and salt, and 12.5 cl water. Cook over low heat for about 10 minutes.

3 Melt the butter in a pan. Stir in the flour and whisk to make a roux. Slowly stir in the milk and heat until the sauce

thickens. Season with salt, pepper, nutmeg and lemon juice. Leave to cool. Whisk two eggs and stir into the sauce.

4 Grease a large ovenproof dish. Line the bottom of the dish with half the macaroni. Sprinkle a little of the grated cheese on top. Rinse the parsley under running water, shake dry and chop finely. Stir the chopped parsley and the remaining egg into the meat, and spread the mixture over the macaroni.

5 Spread the rest of the macaroni on top of the meat, and pour the sauce evenly over the top. Sprinkle with the rest of the cheese. Bake in the centre of the oven for about 45 minutes, until browned. Serve immediately.

Midia me risi

Mussels with rice

Needs care • Ionian Islands

Serves 4

1.5 kg fresh mussels or clams
2 onions (about 200 g)
2 garlic cloves • 3 tbsp olive oil
40 cl dry white wine
½ bay leaf
1 tsp black peppercorns
salt • 30 g parsley
200 g tomatoes
40 g butter
1 tsp tomato purée
sugar
freshly ground black pepper
½ tsp dried oregano
225 g long-grain rice

Preparation time: 1¼ hours

2,400 kJ/570 calories per portion

1 Scrub the mussels or clams under running water; remove the beards with the blunt edge of a knife. Tap any open shells and if they don't close, discard them. Peel and halve 1 onion and 1 garlic clove; heat the oil in a large pan and fry until transparent. Add ¼ litre of the wine, ½ litre water, the bay leaf, peppercorns, salt and 3 parsley sprigs. Bring to the boil.

2 Add the mussels, cover, and cook over high heat for 5 minutes, until they open; discard any that remain closed. Strain the stock and reserve. Peel and chop the remaining onion and garlic clove. Briefly plunge the tomatoes in boiling water, skin and dice them.

3 In a heavy pan, fry the onion and garlic in the butter until transparent. Stir in the tomatoes and tomato purée, and cook briefly. Add the rest of the wine and ¾ litre of the mussel stock. Bring to the boil, and season with salt, a little sugar, ground pepper and the oregano. Stir in the rice, again bring to the boil and cook over low heat for 25 minutes, stirring from time to time. Add more stock, or water, as necessary.

4 Reserve a few whole mussels for the garnish, and remove the rest from their shells. Chop the remaining parsley, and stir it into the rice together with the shelled mussels. Serve, garnished with the reserved mussels.

Giouvetsi me kritharaki

Lamb stew with orzo pasta

Not difficult • Mediterranean islands

Serves 4

700 g leg of lamb
200 g onions • 3 garlic cloves
500 g ripe beef tomatoes
40 g butter
1 tbsp tomato purée
4 tbsp olive oil
1 tsp mild paprika
1 tsp dried thyme
salt • freshly ground black pepper
200 g kritharaki, or orzo (see page 75)
100 g grated kefalograviera or Gruyère cheese

Preparation time: 45 minutes (plus 1½ hours' cooking time)

2,600 kJ/620 calories per portion

1 Preheat the oven to 220°C (425°F or Mark 7). Cut the lamb into 3 cm cubes. Peel the onions and the garlic and dice finely. Plunge the tomatoes briefly into boiling water and skin. Dice the flesh.

2 Heat the butter in a fireproof casserole over high heat and fry the meat until browned. Add the onion and garlic and fry until transparent. Stir in the diced tomato and continue to cook over medium heat for about 5 minutes. Mix the tomato purée with ¼ litre hot water and stir it into the meat. Add the paprika and thyme and season with salt and pepper. Cover, and cook in the centre of the oven for about 1 hour.

3 After an hour, stir in ¾ litre lightly salted water and the *kritharaki*. Return the stew to the oven and cook for a further 30 minutes, stirring from time to time, and adding a little more liquid if necessary. Season with salt and pepper, sprinkle with the grated cheese and serve immediately.

Wine: A retsina, or an unresinated dry red or white wine such as Demestika, goes well with this dish.

Note: If you prefer, you can fry the meat and vegetables in a large frying pan and transfer them to an ovenproof dish before cooking in the oven.

Pasta

The love of pasta is not confined to Italy; many countries of the eastern Mediterranean enjoy this staple as part of their everyday diet. Making fresh pasta at home is a skilful art that requires a lot of patience; in many Greek villages, women carry out the task together. However, good dried Greek pasta is readily available in specialist food shops.

This pasta comes in a range of shapes. Typically Greek is the tiny tear-shaped *kritharaki*, or orzo, which resembles rice; handfuls of it are added to stews or cooked with rice, sometimes lightly toasted in hot fat beforehand. Also popular are the little squares known as *hylopittes*, or "thousand breads".

Greece's pasta dishes, like much of the country's cuisine, reflect a variety of cultural influences; *kritharaki* is thought to have originated in Asia; and the famous meat and macaroni pie *pastitsio* was brought to Greece by the Venetians and the Genoese, who for a period of 500 years held sway over the larger islands in the Aegean and Mediterranean.

Spanakorizo

Spinach and rice

Not difficult • Attica

Serves 4

1 kg leaf spinach
200 g spring onions
30 g dill
5 tbsp olive oil
120 g long-grain rice
salt
freshly ground black pepper
1 unwaxed lemon

Preparation time: 45 minutes

1,100 kJ/260 calories per portion

1 Thoroughly wash the spinach, remove stalks and any hard ribs and cut it into narrow strips. Wash and trim the spring onions, removing any coarse outer leaves, and slice thinly. Rinse the dill under running water, shake dry and chop finely.

2 Heat the olive oil in a large frying pan and fry the spring onion until transparent. Stir in the spinach and cook over medium heat for 3 to 4 minutes until the spinach wilts. Add the rice and 60 cl water, and bring to the boil. Reduce the heat, and stir in the dill, salt and a little pepper.

3 Cover the pan and cook the spinach and rice for about 20 minutes. The finished dish should be moist so, if necessary, add 2 to 3 tbsp water. Adjust the seasoning if required, and serve at once, accompanied by the lemon cut into wedges.

Pastitsio me prassa

Baked macaroni and leeks

Not difficult • Mainland Greece

Serves 4

500 g macaroni
salt
80 g butter
500 g leeks
freshly ground black pepper
500 g ripe tomatoes
1 large chili pepper (see Glossary)
100 g black olives
1 tsp tomato purée
2 eggs
2 tbsp milk
80 g grated kefalograviera or
Gruyère cheese

Preparation time: 1½ hours

1,700 kJ/400 calories per portion

1 Bring a large pan of lightly salted water to the boil and cook the macaroni until *al dente*. Rinse under running water and drain. Line the base of an ovenproof dish with a layer of macaroni. In a little saucepan, melt half the butter until it just begins to turn brown; dribble it over the pasta.

2 Preheat the oven to 200°C (400°F or Mark 6). Trim the leeks, and cut in half lengthwise. Wash, then cut into pieces about 4 cm long. Melt the rest of the butter in a pan and sauté the leeks, covered, over low heat for about 10 minutes. Season with salt and pepper.

3 Spread the leeks on top of the macaroni. Wash and slice the tomatoes and layer them on top of the leeks. Wash the chili pepper and cut it in half lengthwise. Remove the ribs and seeds. Lay the halves of chili on top of the tomato. Rinse the olives and arrange them on top.

4 Dissolve the tomato purée in ½ cup hot water and pour over the pie. Bake in the centre of the oven for about 45 minutes. About 10 minutes before the end of the cooking time, whisk together the eggs and milk and pour them over the pie. Top with the grated cheese, and bake for a further 10 minutes.

Variation:
Prassaoryzo (Leeks with rice)
Cut 1 kg leeks into pieces, 200 g carrots into matchsticks and dice 1 onion. Sauté in 4 tbsp olive oil over medium heat, uncovered, for 5 minutes. Add 50 g rice, 30 cl water, salt and a little sugar and pepper. Cover, and cook over low heat for about 40 minutes. Season with 1 tbsp lemon juice. Serve warm.

Hylopittes metsovou

Metsovo-style pasta squares

Needs care • Northern Greece

Serves 4 to 6

For the pasta:
500 g flour, plus flour for rolling
salt
2 tbsp olive oil
2 eggs

For the sauce:
300 g rindless, lean bacon
200 g onions
2 garlic cloves
1 stick celery
400 g tomatoes
3 tbsp olive oil
salt
freshly ground black pepper
100 g grated kefalograviera or
Gruyère cheese

Preparation time: about 2 hours
(plus 1 hour's standing time)

2,700 kJ/640 calories per portion
(if serving 6)

1 Sift the flour and 1 tsp salt into a bowl. Make a well in the centre of the flour and pour in the olive oil, eggs and 15 cl warm water. Knead to a smooth dough. Continue kneading for at least 10 minutes, then wrap tightly in foil. Leave to stand for about 1 hour.

2 Roll the dough into a thick sausage, and divide it into six to eight portions. Take one portion and rewrap the remainder to prevent the dough from drying out. On a floured work surface, roll the dough out very thinly, keeping both it and the work surface well-sprinkled with flour to stop it sticking.

3 Sprinkle the sheet of dough with a little flour and fold it in half (*above*); do not allow the halves to stick together.

4 With a sharp knife, cut the dough into 1 cm squares (*above*) then, with the knife, carefully separate the two layers.

5 Spread the pasta squares on a dry tea towel. Repeat the procedure with the remaining portions of dough.

6 Finely dice the bacon. Peel and finely dice the onions and the garlic. Rinse the celery under running water, cut into dice and chop the leaves.

7 Plunge the tomatoes briefly into boiling water, skin them and dice the flesh. Heat the oil in a frying pan, and brown the bacon over medium heat.

8 Add the onions, garlic and celery and stir-fry for about 1 minute. Stir in the tomatoes and continue to cook for a further minute. Season with salt and pepper.

9 Bring a large pan of lightly salted water to the boil. Add the pasta and boil briskly for about 3 minutes. Drain, and place on a warmed serving dish. Pour the hot bacon sauce over the pasta and sprinkle with grated cheese. Serve immediately.

Wine: A strong dry red Naoussa from northern Greece is an excellent accompaniment to this dish.

Note: To stop the pasta sticking together, you can, if you like, add a few drops of oil to the cooking water.

FISH AND SEAFOOD

T he waters of the Mediterranean have always yielded a bounty of fresh fish and shellfish, an inspiration for the Greek love of seafood. The year-round harvest of the fishermen forms the basis of a simple but hearty cuisine, which uses characteristic Greek ingredients to produce a range of traditional dishes.

The fish, for example, might be simply marinated in herbs and lemon juice before grilling or baking; sautéed with tomatoes, onions, garlic, olive oil and wine; stuffed with a filling of rice, raisins and pine-nuts; or deep fried or baked in the oven with vegetables and ewe's cheese. Squid appears cooked in a rich tomato sauce, in its own ink, or baked in a fish pie with vegetables. Many recipes can be easily adapted to a wide range of different fish—you can experiment for yourself.

Particularly prized in Greece are members of the sea bream family (*see page 83*), whilst cooks also like to keep a supply of dried octopus and squid: lines of octopuses, hung out to dry like washing, are a familiar sight in mainland or island resorts. Each evening, as the day's catch is prepared in homes and tavernas, those towns fill with a mouth-watering perfume of rosemary and bay leaves, and the aroma of grilled fish.

Lithrini fourno ala spetsiota

Not difficult • Spetses **Baked sea bream** *Serves 4*

2 cleaned red sea bream (about 600 g each)
salt
freshly ground black pepper
juice of 1 lemon
2 small sprigs fresh rosemary
1 bunch spring onions or 2 medium-sized onions (about 200 g)
2 garlic cloves
200 g ripe tomatoes
30 g parsley
4 tbsp olive oil
12.5 cl dry white wine
2 tbsp fresh breadcrumbs
50 g feta cheese

Preparation time:
45 minutes

1,500 kJ/360 calories per portion

1 Preheat the oven to 200°C (400°F or Mark 6). Rinse the fish inside and out under cold running water and pat dry. Make two diagonal incisions on either side of the fish, in the thickest part.

2 Sprinkle the fish inside and out with a little salt and pepper and the lemon juice. Place a sprig of rosemary in the body cavities, and lay the fish in a roasting pan.

3 Trim and wash the spring onions and cut into pieces about 5 cm long; if using ordinary onions, peel and slice them. Peel and crush the garlic. Plunge the tomatoes briefly in boiling water, skin them, then dice the flesh. Wash the parsley, shake dry and chop finely.

4 Heat 3 tbsp of the olive oil in a frying pan over medium heat. Add the onions and garlic, and fry until transparent. Stir in the tomatoes and parsley, and cook for 2 minutes more. Add the wine and bring the sauce briefly to the boil. Season with salt and pepper, and pour over the fish. Sprinkle with the breadcrumbs and the remaining oil.

5 Cook in the centre of the oven for about 15 minutes. Dice the feta cheese and sprinkle it over the fish. Return to the oven and cook for a further 10 minutes. Serve hot.

Wine: A strong retsina goes well with this hearty dish.

Note: Gilt-head bream, dentex or redfish are good alternatives.

The sea bream family

In Greece, as throughout the Mediterranean, bream are among the most prized fish for their firm, lean flesh. Of the 20 or so species of bream native to the Mediterranean, perhaps the most delicious are the gilt-head bream, so called because of the distinctive gold crescent between its eyes, and the dentex, which has a strikingly high forehead. Also excellent are the pandora which, unlike many of its silvery-grey relatives, is a glossy red, and the saddled bream. The red sea bream is one of the few sea breams also found in northern European waters.

Bream live at depths of between 20 and 30 metres among the weeds and rocks on the bottom of the sea, where they feed on crabs and other seabed creatures. Greek fishermen catch them by day and by night with nets or bait dangling on long, thin lines, attached to floating, anchored rafts known as *paraketa*. Once caught, these highly adaptable fish can be prepared in many imaginative and delicious ways: simply grilled, fried or baked, or stewed with other ingredients such as onions, tomatoes, olive oil, wine and herbs.

Oktapodi krassato

Fairly easy • Cyclades | **Octopus in wine** | *Serves 4*

1 octopus (about 800 g), whole or ready-cleaned
salt
200 g onions
300 g ripe tomatoes
60 g fennel leaves or dill
1 tbsp tomato purée
4 tbsp olive oil
20 cl dry red wine
freshly ground black pepper

Preparation time: 1½ hours

1,200 kJ/290 calories per portion

1 Rinse the octopus in running water. If not already prepared, cut off the head between the body pouch and the tentacles (*above*) and discard.

2 Pull the skin away from the body pouch (*above*), and discard.

3 Turn the body pouch inside out, remove the viscera (*above*) and ink sac. Wash inside and out thoroughly.

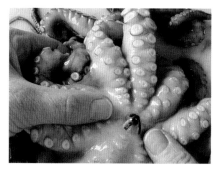

4 Press out the beak at the base of the tentacles (*above*).

5 Heat a large, dry, non-stick frying pan over medium heat. Place the octopus tentacles and pouch in the pan, sprinkle with a little salt and cook in its own juices for about 15 minutes, turning once.

6 Meanwhile, peel and halve the onions, then cut lengthwise into slices or strips. Plunge the tomatoes briefly in boiling water, skin and slice them. Wash the fennel or dill, shake dry and cut into several pieces. Dissolve the tomato purée in 12.5 cl water. Remove the octopus from the pan, rinse under lukewarm running water and drain.

7 Cut the tentacles and pouch into bite-sized pieces. Heat the olive oil in a heavy saucepan. Add the onions and fry over medium heat until transparent. Add the octopus, and toss in the pan for about 30 seconds. Stir in the tomato purée, wine and a little salt and pepper, and bring to the boil.

8 Arrange the tomatoes and fennel on top of the other ingredients, shake lightly and cover. Cook over low heat for 50 minutes to 1 hour, until tender. Check for seasoning and serve hot or warm with fresh crusty bread.

Souvlakia psaria

Not difficult • Dodecanese

Fish kebabs

Serves 4

800 g redfish fillets
4 tbsp olive oil
juice of ½ lemon
2 sprigs fresh thyme
1 small sprig fresh rosemary
100 g shallots
200 g tomatoes
200 g small courgettes
150 g sweet peppers
salt
freshly ground black pepper
30 g flat-leaf parsley

Preparation time: 1 hour

1,400 kJ/330 calories per portion

1 Wash the fish under cold running water, pat dry and cut into cubes or slices about 3 cm long. In a bowl, mix the olive oil and lemon juice together. Wash the thyme and rosemary, shake dry, chop the leaves and stir into the bowl. Coat the fish in the marinade and leave to stand for about 30 minutes.

2 Meanwhile, peel and halve the shallots. Wash the tomatoes and cut into quarters. Rinse the courgettes under running water, trim and cut into 2 cm thick slices. Wash and halve the sweet peppers, and remove the white ribs and seeds. Cut the flesh crosswise into rings or strips about 2 cm wide.

3 Preheat the grill. Drain any excess marinade from the fish pieces, then thread them onto long wooden skewers, alternating with pieces of vegetable. Place under the grill for 2 to 3 minutes on each side, until slightly browned. Sprinkle with salt and pepper. Rinse and dry the parsley, arrange on a dish, place the kebabs on top and serve.

Wine: Choose a dry white wine, for example from the island of Euboea.

Note: Fish kebabs are delicious grilled over charcoal. If you prefer, fry them in 3 tbsp olive oil over medium heat in a large pan for 2 minutes on each side.

Xiphios marinatos

Not difficult • Crete

Marinated swordfish

Serves 4

4 medium-sized, 1.5 cm-thick
swordfish steaks (about 250 g each)
juice of 1 lemon
8 tbsp olive oil
30 g parsley
2 sprigs fresh thyme
1 lemon
200 g red onions
400 g tomatoes
400 g small, crisp cucumbers
8 bay leaves
salt
freshly ground black pepper

Preparation time: 45 minutes
(plus 1 hour's marinating time)

990 kJ/240 calories per portion

1 Rinse the fish under cold running water and pat dry. Place the lemon juice and 4 tbsp of the oil in a small bowl. Wash and dry the parsley. Finely chop the leaves and stir into the bowl. Brush the fish steaks on both sides with the sauce, stack on top of each other in the bowl and leave to marinate for about 1 hour, turning once.

2 Meanwhile, wash the thyme, shake dry and tear off the leaves. Wash the lemon and cut into quarters. Peel the onions and cut them lengthwise into quarters. Wash and slice the tomatoes. Peel the cucumbers and cut lengthwise into quarters.

3 Remove the fish from the bowl, reserving any remaining marinade. If you have a frying pan large enough to hold all four fish steaks, heat the remaining olive oil in it. Add the bay leaves and fish, and fry over medium heat for about 2 minutes. Sprinkle with thyme. Turn the fish and fry for about 2 minutes on the other side. If using a smaller frying pan, cook the fish in two batches, using 2 tbsp oil and 4 bay leaves each time.

4 Discard the bay leaves. Dribble any remaining marinade over the fish. Sprinkle lightly with salt and pepper. Serve on warmed plates with the sliced vegetables and a wedge of lemon, and accompanied by fresh crusty bread.

Bakaliaros yiahni

Braised salt cod

Not difficult • Mainland Greece   *Serves 4*

1 kg salt cod
2 large onions (about 300 g)
3 garlic cloves
500 g ripe tomatoes
1 tsp tomato purée
5 tbsp olive oil
12.5 cl dry white wine
2 tbsp currants
2 tbsp pine-nuts
3 sprigs fresh mint
freshly ground black pepper
salt

Preparation time: 1¼ hours
(plus 24 hours' soaking time)

4,400 kJ/1,000 calories per portion

1 Cut the cod into three or four pieces. Place in a large bowl of cold water and leave to soak for at least 24 hours, changing the water several times, until the fish has roughly doubled in size.

2 Dry the fish, squeezing out any excess liquid. Remove the skin (*above*) and bones, and cut the flesh into large cubes. Peel the onions and garlic and dice them. Plunge the tomatoes briefly in boiling water, skin them and cut into dice. Stir the tomato purée into 12.5 cl water to dissolve.

3 Heat the olive oil in a large heavy pan over medium heat and fry the onions until transparent. Stir in the tomatoes and sauté for about 1 minute more. Stir in the tomato purée, wine, currants, garlic and pine-nuts, and bring to the boil.

4 Add the fish to the pan, stir, then reduce the heat to low and cook for about 45 minutes, until the sauce thickens. If the liquid evaporates too quickly, add a little water.

5 Meanwhile, rinse the mint under cold running water and coarsely chop the leaves. Season the fish with pepper and a very little salt. Stir the mint into the sauce and serve.

Wine: A well-chilled retsina is the ideal accompaniment for this dish.

Variation: Salt cod balls
Soak the fish pieces for at least 24 hours. Squeeze out any excess liquid, remove the skin and bones, and cut into bite-sized pieces. Make a smooth batter from 100 g flour, 1 egg, 1 tbsp oil, white pepper, salt and 12.5 cl water. Dip the fish in the batter to coat, deep fry, sprinkle with lemon juice and serve with *skordalia me patates*, or garlic and potato purée (*page 43*).

Note: Although cod is not found in the Mediterranean, salt cod has been imported from Scandinavia since the Middle Ages. Nowadays, the Greeks, like their neighbours, obtain most of their salt cod from Norway and Iceland.

When you buy salt cod, it should be off-white or greyish in colour. A dull, yellow colour indicates that the fish has been left in salt for too long. When soaked in cold water, the fish regains its original plumpness, tenderness and white colour, and can be prepared in any of the ways suitable for fresh fish.

Allow at least a day for soaking before use; to remove the briny taste completely, soak for 48 hours. Always take care when adding salt during cooking or at table.

Palamida plaki

Bonito with vegetables

Fairly easy • Aegean Islands

Serves 4

1 kg bonito or tuna cutlets
200 g onions
2 garlic cloves
200 g waxy potatoes
200 g carrots
2 sticks celery
30 g parsley
300 g tomatoes
5 tbsp olive oil
12.5 cl dry white wine
salt
freshly ground black pepper
juice of ½ lemon
1 lemon

Preparation time:
1¼ hours

3,200 kJ/760 calories
per portion

1 Rinse the fish under cold running water and pat dry. Peel the onions and garlic. Cut the onions into rings and the garlic into thin slices. Peel the potatoes and carrots and cut into medium-sized cubes. Trim and wash the celery and cut into small pieces. Rinse the parsley, shake dry and coarsely chop the leaves. Plunge the tomatoes briefly in boiling water, skin them and cut into dice.

2 Heat the olive oil in a large sauté pan or deep frying pan over medium heat. Fry the onions and garlic until transparent. Stir in the potatoes, carrots, celery and tomatoes and cook for about 10 minutes, shaking the pan from time to time. Add the wine to the pan, bring to the boil, and season with salt and pepper.

3 Arrange the fish cutlets in the pan and sprinkle over the parsley and lemon juice. Cover the pan and cook over low heat for about 20 minutes. Wash the lemon, cut it into quarters and serve with the fish.

Wine: This dish goes well with a fruity, dry white Robola from Kephalonia.

Variation:
Bonito with vegetables and olives
Preheat the oven to 180°C (350°F or Mark 4). Cook the vegetables as in Steps 1 and 2 above. Arrange with the fish in a roasting pan or baking dish and cook in the centre of the oven for about 35 minutes. Ten minutes before the end of cooking time, sprinkle with 100 g stoned black olives.

Kalamarakia yemisto

Takes a little time • Athens
Stuffed squid

Serves 4

4 medium-sized squid (about
700 g), preferably cleaned
200 g onions
1 sprig fresh mint
6 tbsp olive oil
3 tbsp pine-nuts
2 tbsp small currants
80 g long-grain rice
salt
freshly ground black pepper
cinnamon
paprika
12.5 cl dry red wine
honey
15 g flat-leaf parsley
30 g dill

Preparation time:
1½ hours

1,500 kJ/360 calories
per portion

1 If the squid have not been cleaned, pull the head and tentacles away from the body pouches. Remove the pens, or quills, and ink sacs. Sever the heads and viscera from the tentacles and discard. Squeeze out the beaks from the tentacles and discard. Skin the pouches and wash inside and out under running water. Rinse the tentacles and cut into small pieces.

2 Peel and finely chop the onions. Wash, dry and finely chop the mint. In a sauté or heavy pan, heat 3 tbsp of the oil and fry half the onions until transparent. Add the squid tentacles and fry briefly. Stir in the pine-nuts, currants and rice and cook, shaking the pan, for about 1 minute. Stir in a little salt, pepper, cinnamon and paprika, and the mint. Add just enough water to cover the ingredients. Cover and cook over low heat for about 15 minutes, then leave to cool.

3 Spoon the rice mixture into the squid pouches and secure the open ends with toothpicks. Heat the remaining oil in the pan over medium heat and fry the rest of the onions. Add the red wine and 12.5 cl water, bring to the boil and season with salt and pepper and a little honey. Arranged the stuffed pouches in the pan, cover and cook over low heat for 50 minutes to 1 hour, until tender enough to be pierced with a sharp knife. If the liquid evaporates too quickly, add a little hot water.

4 Meanwhile, wash the parsley and dill, and shake dry. Reserve a few leaves of each, coarsely chop the rest and sprinkle over the pouches about 5 minutes before the end of the cooking time. Serve garnished with the reserved parsley and dill, and accompanied by fresh crusty bread.

Note: Squid are available deep-frozen.

Sardelles sto fourno

Baked sardines

Not difficult • Cyclades

Serves 4

1 kg fresh sardines
salt
5 garlic cloves
60 g parsley
4 tbsp olive oil
juice of 1 lemon
1 tsp dried oregano
freshly ground black pepper

Preparation time: about 50 minutes

1,600 kJ/380 calories per portion

1 If the sardines have not already been cleaned, scale them using the blunt edge of a small kitchen knife, working from the tail towards the head (*above*). Take care not to damage the skin.

2 Cut off the heads. Slit open along the bellies; gut them and remove the tails and backbones. Thoroughly wash the fish under running water and pat dry.

3 Preheat the oven to 180°C (350°F or Mark 4). Lightly sprinkle the insides of the sardines with salt, then lay them side by side in an ovenproof dish. Peel and thinly slice the garlic. Wash the parsley under running water, shake dry and chop the leaves. Place half the parsley in a small bowl with the garlic and reserve the rest.

4 Add the oil, lemon juice, a little salt, the oregano, and a generous pinch of pepper to the parsley and garlic in the bowl. Stir thoroughly and dribble the mixture over the fish, at the same time inserting a few slices of garlic between the fish.

5 Bake in the centre of the oven until the fish can be easily pierced with a fork, about 20 to 30 minutes depending on their size. Sprinkle the reserved chopped parsley over the top and serve with fresh, crusty bread.

Wine: The distinctive flavour of a dry white Thira wine from the volcanic island of Santorini goes very well with baked sardines.

Variation: Fried sardines
Prepare the sardines as described in Steps 1 and 2 above. Peel and chop 2 cloves of garlic. Slice 3 tomatoes. Heat 4 tbsp olive oil in a frying pan, and fry the garlic over a medium heat until translucent. Lay the sardines side by side in the pan. Sprinkle with salt, pepper and 30 g chopped parsley, and top with the tomato. Pour over 12.5 cl white wine or water and the juice of ½ lemon. Cover the pan and cook the fish over medium heat for 10 to 15 minutes, shaking from time to time. Serve with fresh, crusty bread.

VEGETABLES

W hether combined with pasta
or rice, used to fill pasties
and pies, or simply prepared
to accompany meat, vegetables dishes in
Greece are fit for a king. A day without
vegetables is unthinkable when the
mainland and the islands yield such a
rich harvest of edible, natural treasures.

In spring and early summer, when
the valleys, plains and lower mountain
slopes are cloaked in luxuriant green,
men and women alike compete with
sheep and goats to find such tender
wild plants as slender asparagus, tasty
young cardoons—spiky relations of the
artichoke—and small onions. Business
is brisk in the markets as the Greeks
take full advantage of this bounty,
which they transform into exquisite
dishes, sometimes using unusual,
imaginative combinations, such as
artichokes, broad beans and carrots.

Greece's natural riches have long
played an important part in a tradition
of vegetarian cookery encouraged by
religious considerations. Almost a third
of the church calendar consists of fast
days on which no meat—or, strictly
speaking, anything that bleeds, including
eggs or fish—can be eaten. During these
times, which are still widely observed
on the islands and in rural areas of the
mainland, squid and other shellfish are
popular, and vegetables come into their
own. But even without such a custom,
few in Greece would wish to do without
their remarkable vegetable dishes.

Briami

Vegetable bake

Simple • Ionian Islands

Serves 4

300 g medium-sized aubergines
salt
200 g courgettes
200 g waxy potatoes
200 g onions
2 garlic cloves
250 g fresh or frozen green beans
300 g ripe tomatoes
10 cl olive oil
freshly ground black pepper
sugar
15 g flat-leaf parsley
feta cheese

Preparation time: 2 hours

1,400 kJ/330 calories per portion

1 Wash the aubergines, trim the stalks and cut crosswise into 5 mm-thick slices. Place in a bowl of cold, salted water for about 20 minutes to draw out any bitter juices. Trim, wash and dry the courgettes, and slice them.

2 Peel and thinly slice the potatoes and onions. Peel and finely chop the garlic. If using fresh green beans, rinse and pat them dry. Trim and string them, then cut into pieces 3 to 4 cm long. Wash and slice the tomatoes.

3 Preheat the oven to 180°C (350°F or Mark 4). Drain the aubergines and pat dry. In a large frying pan, heat the oil over high heat and fry the aubergines, turning once, until lightly browned on both sides. Place in a colander or sieve over a bowl and press with the back of a large spoon to drain, reserving the oil.

4 Arrange the sliced aubergines in a layer in a deep ovenproof dish. Lightly seasoning between each layer with a little salt, pepper and sugar, place the other vegetables on top, ending with a layer of tomato slices.

5 Mix the reserved oil with 12.5 cl hot water and pour over the vegetables. Cover the dish with aluminium foil and bake in the centre of the oven for about 30 minutes. Remove the foil and bake uncovered for a further 30 minutes. Meanwhile, wash the parsley, pat dry and chop finely. Sprinkle over the baked vegetables and serve hot, accompanied by slices of feta cheese and fresh, crusty bread.

Domates ke piperies yemistes
Stuffed vegetables

Takes a little time • Mainland Greece

Serves 4

4 large beef tomatoes (about 600 g)
4 large sweet green or red peppers
(about 500 g)
sugar
salt
freshly ground black pepper
400 g waxy potatoes
15 g parsley
2 sprigs fresh mint
80 g long-grain rice
1 large onion
8 tbsp olive oil
300 g minced beef
paprika
3 tbsp tomato purée

Preparation time: 2 hours

*2,100 kJ/500 calories
per portion*

1 Wash the tomatoes and sweet peppers. Carefully slice off the tops and set aside. With a spoon, scoop out and reserve the tomato pulp. Trim the ribs from the peppers and rinse out the seeds. Sprinkle the insides of the tomatoes with a little sugar, salt and black pepper, and the peppers with salt and black pepper. Peel the potatoes, cut into thick sticks and place in a bowl of cold water. Wash the parsley and mint, pat dry and chop finely.

2 In a bowl of lukewarm water, soak the rice for about 15 minutes. Peel the onion and chop very finely. Heat 4 tbsp of the oil in a sauté pan or heavy saucepan over medium heat and fry the onion until transparent. Stir in the beef and cook, stirring from time to time, until all the meat juices evaporate.

3 Chop the tomato pulp and stir into the pan. Season with salt, pepper and a little paprika. Drain the rice, and stir into the pan with 12.5 cl water. Reduce the heat to low, cover the pan and simmer for about 10 minutes.

4 Meanwhile, preheat the oven to 180°C (350°F or Mark 4). Stir the parsley and mint into the rice mixture, then carefully spoon the mixture into the tomatoes and peppers. Cover with the reserved tops and arrange in an ovenproof dish.

5 Drain the potatoes, pat dry and arrange them between the tomatoes and peppers. Mix the tomato purée with the remaining oil and 25 cl hot water, and pour over the vegetables. Bake in the centre of the oven for about 1 hour. Serve straight from the dish.

Anginares me koukia

More complex • Crete   **Artichokes and broad beans**   *Serves 4*

juice of 1 lemon
4 medium-sized young artichokes
(about 600 g)
500 g young, tender broad beans
300 g carrots
300 g waxy potatoes
1 leafy fennel bulb
1 medium-sized onion
4 tbsp olive oil
salt
freshly ground black pepper
3 egg yolks
juice of 1 lemon

Preparation time: 1½ hours

1,200 kJ/290 calories per portion

1 Put about 3 litres water in a pan and add the lemon juice. Pull off the tough outer leaves from each artichoke and trim the tips of the rest. Halve lengthwise and remove the purple leaves and hairy chokes. Thinly peel the stalks. As soon as each artichoke is trimmed, put it in the water. Bring the water to the boil and cook the artichokes for 20 to 25 minutes. Drain and leave to cool, then cut into slices.

2 Meanwhile, wash the broad beans and pat dry; trim and string. Remove the beans from the larger pods; leave the smaller pods whole. Peel the carrots and potatoes and cut into large pieces. Wash and trim the fennel, reserving the leaves for garnish. Cut the bulb into thin strips. In a large pan,

bring 1 litre water to the boil and cook the beans, potatoes, carrots and fennel for about 15 minutes. Drain through a colander, reserving the cooking water.

3 Peel and dice the onion. In a large pan, heat the oil and sauté the onion until transparent. Stir in the artichokes and other vegetables and cook over medium heat for about 2 minutes. Add 50 cl of the vegetable water and cook for a further 8 minutes.

4 Season with salt and pepper, remove from the heat and allow to cool. Whisk together the egg yolks and lemon juice and stir into the pan. Reheat, stirring constantly, until the sauce thickens; do not let it boil, otherwise it will curdle. Serve, garnished with the fennel leaves.

Anginares me spanaki

More complex • Athens   **Artichoke and spinach bake**   *Serves 4*

juice of 1 lemon
8 small, long artichokes
(about 800 g)
1 kg leaf spinach
200 g cooked ham
200 g kefalograviera cheese
85 g butter • salt
1 heaped tbsp flour
25 cl milk
freshly ground black pepper
1 egg
100 g grated kefalotyri or
Parmesan cheese

Preparation time: 1¾ hours

2,900 kJ/690 calories per portion

1 Put 3 litres water In a large pan and add the lemon juice. Wash, prepare and cut the artichokes in half as in Step 1 above and add to the pan. Bring the water to the boil, cover and cook over medium heat for 15 to 20 minutes, until tender. Drain, leave to cool and slice. Meanwhile, wash and dry the spinach, and cut into 1 cm-wide strips. Dice the ham and *kefalograviera* cheese.

2 Butter an ovenproof dish. In a frying pan, heat half the butter and fry the artichokes until browned. Remove from the pan and layer in the dish. Season with a little salt and sprinkle over half the diced ham and cheese. In the butter

left in the pan, cook the spinach with a little salt until it wilts. Arrange in a layer in the dish and top with the rest of the ham and cheese.

3 Preheat the oven to 220°C (425°F or Mark 7). Heat the remaining butter in a pan, add the flour and cook briefly, stirring, until brown. Stir in the milk and bring to the boil over high heat. Cook for 5 to 8 minutes, stirring, until the sauce thickens. Remove from the heat; season with salt and pepper. Whisk the egg and stir into the sauce. Pour over the dish, and top with the grated cheese. Bake in the centre of the oven for 20 to 30 minutes, until browned. Serve at once.

Moussaka
Aubergines baked with meat

Serves 4 to 6

800 g aubergines • salt
200 g onions • 600 g tomatoes
25 cl olive oil
600 g minced beef
25 cl dry white wine
¼ tsp sugar
½ tsp ground cinnamon
freshly ground black pepper
30 g parsley
1 small sprig fresh, or 1 tsp dried,
oregano
100 g grated kefalograviera or
Parmesan cheese
100 g fresh breadcrumbs
40 g butter • 4 tbsp flour
75 cl milk • freshly grated nutmeg
2 tsp lemon juice • 3 eggs

Preparation time: 2 hours
(including soaking time)

4,100 kJ/980 calories per portion
(if serving 6)

1 Wash the aubergines under running water. Trim off the stalks and cut the aubergines crosswise into 5 mm-thick slices. Place in a bowl of cold, salted water for about 20 minutes, then drain and pat dry with kitchen paper.

2 Meanwhile, peel and dice the onions. Plunge the tomatoes briefly into boiling water and skin them. Dice the flesh.

3 Heat 3 to 4 tbsp of the olive oil in a large, non-stick frying pan. Fry the aubergine in batches over high heat until lightly browned on both sides, adding more oil as necessary. Drain on kitchen paper and reserve. In the oil left in the pan, fry the onions until

transparent. Stir in the minced beef and fry over high heat until all the cooking juices have evaporated.

4 Stir in the tomatoes, white wine, salt, sugar, cinnamon and pepper. Cover the pan and cook over medium heat for about 5 minutes. Meanwhile, wash and dry the parsley and the fresh oregano, if using. Tear off the leaves and chop them. Stir the parsley and fresh or dried oregano into the meat, cook for 5 minutes more, then leave to cool.

5 Preheat the oven to 180°C (350°F or Mark 4). Stir half the cheese and about 2 tbsp of breadcrumbs into the meat.

6 In a small saucepan, melt the butter, reserving a little. Stir in the flour and cook briefly until lightly brown. Slowly stir in the milk, and bring to the boil. Cook for 5 to 8 minutes, stirring constantly, until the sauce thickens. Season with salt, pepper, nutmeg and lemon juice, then allow to cool slightly.

7 Whisk 2 of the eggs and stir into the sauce with the remaining cheese. Butter a baking dish and line with the rest of the breadcrumbs. Stir the remaining egg into the meat. Arrange half the aubergines in a layer in the dish. Cover with the meat mixture. Top with the rest of the aubergines, and pour over the sauce. Bake in the centre of the oven for about 1 hour, then cut into squares and serve.

Wine: A potent red Mavroudi from central Greece is a good choice.

Note: Moussaka can also be made with other vegetables such as courgettes, tomatoes, potatoes or green beans. Courgettes and potatoes should be sliced and fried first, and beans should be blanched.

Prassa yiahni

Braised leeks

Simple • Central Greece

Serves 4

600 g leeks
200 g carrots
1 stick celery
1 onion
400 g tomatoes
3 tbsp olive oil
5 cm piece cinnamon stick
1 bay leaf
2 tbsp red wine vinegar
salt
sugar
freshly ground black pepper

Preparation time: 1½ hours

550 kJ/130 calories per portion

1 Trim the leeks and halve lengthwise. Wash thoroughly under cold running water. Cut into pieces about 2 cm long.

2 Peel the carrots and cut into 2 cm pieces. Trim the celery, reserving the leaves, and wash under cold running water. Cut crosswise into thin slices, and coarsely chop the leaves. Peel and dice the onion.

3 Plunge the tomatoes briefly into boiling water; skin and halve them. Dice the flesh. Heat the olive oil in a heavy saucepan over low heat. Add the leeks, carrots, celery and onion, and sauté, uncovered, for about 10 minutes, stirring occasionally.

4 Stir in the tomatoes, then add the cinnamon, bay leaf and wine vinegar, and a little salt and sugar. Season generously with black pepper and stir in 30 cl hot water. Cover and cook over low heat for about 50 minutes, stirring from time to time, until the vegetables are tender. Allow to cool a little. Remove the cinnamon and bay leaf and serve as a main dish.

Bamies laderes

Okra in tomato sauce

Not difficult • Athens

Serves 4

700 g small okra, about 3 to 5 cm long
12.5 cl wine vinegar
200 g onions
3 garlic cloves
400 g ripe tomatoes
6 tbsp olive oil
salt
sugar
freshly ground black pepper
30 g flat-leaf parsley

Preparation time: 1 hour
(plus 1 hour's soaking time)

910 kJ/220 calories per portion

1 Using a small, sharp knife, trim the stalks from the okra, taking care not to damage the pods. Place in a bowl with the wine vinegar and enough cold water to cover. Leave to soak for about 1 hour.

2 Meanwhile, peel and finely dice the onions and garlic. Plunge the tomatoes briefly into boiling water, skin them and dice the flesh. Heat the olive oil in a heavy saucepan over medium heat and sauté the onions and garlic until transparent.

3 Transfer the okra to a colander, wash under cold running water and leave to drain. Put the okra in the pan and cook for about 3 minutes more, stirring constantly. Stir in the tomatoes. Season with a little salt and sugar, and a generous amount of black pepper.

4 Stir in 12.5 cl water and simmer over low heat for about 30 minutes, until the okra is tender. Meanwhile, wash the parsley under running water and shake dry. Chop the leaves and stir into the vegetables. Serve hot or warm as an accompaniment to grilled meat or fish, or as a main course with rice or fresh, crusty bread.

Kolokithakia avgolemono
Courgettes with egg and lemon sauce

More complex • Mainland Greece

Serves 4

4 large courgettes (about 1 kg)
150 g onions
4 tbsp olive oil
80 g long-grain rice
salt
freshly ground black pepper
paprika
15 g flat-leaf parsley
3 sprigs fresh mint
2 eggs
juice of 1 lemon

Preparation time: 1½ hours

930 kJ/220 calories per portion

1 Wash and trim the courgettes. Cut in half crosswise and scoop out the flesh with a teaspoon, leaving a fairly thick casing. Finely chop the flesh. Peel and finely dice the onions.

2 Heat the oil in a pan over medium heat, fry the onions until transparent, then stir in the courgette flesh and the rice. Fry until the rice is transparent, then add 15 cl water and a little salt, pepper and paprika. Cover and cook over low heat for about 10 minutes.

3 Wash and dry the parsley and mint. Chop the leaves, reserving 1 sprig of mint for garnish, and stir into the rice. Season with salt. Spoon the rice mixture into the courgette cases, pressing firmly to fill. Lay them side by side in a heavy pan, add 75 cl hot, salted water and cook, covered, over low heat for 30 to 40 minutes.

4 Drain the courgettes, reserving the water in a small pan, and keep warm. Whisk the eggs with the lemon juice. Top up the courgette water to make 75 cl. Stir in the whisked eggs and heat the sauce, stirring constantly, until it thickens. Pour over the courgettes. Serve garnished with mint.

Papoutsakia
"Little shoes"

Takes a little time • Mainland Greece

Serves 4

4 medium-sized aubergines
(about 1 kg)
4 tbsp olive oil
1 large onion
300 g beef tomatoes
30 g parsley
300 g minced beef or lamb
1 tbsp tomato purée • salt
freshly ground black pepper
2 tbsp fresh breadcrumbs
100 g grated kefalotyri, or
Emmenthal, cheese
40 g butter
2 tbsp flour
50 cl milk • 2 tbsp lemon juice
freshly grated nutmeg
1 egg

Preparation time: 1¾ hours

2,500 kJ/600 calories per portion

1 Wash and dry the aubergines, and cut off the stalks. Heat the oil in a frying pan over high heat and brown the aubergines on all sides. Remove— reserving the pan and oil—and allow to cool, then halve lengthwise and scoop out the flesh, leaving a thin shell. Chop the flesh and set aside.

2 Peel and finely dice the onion. Plunge the tomatoes in boiling water, skin and halve them. Dice the flesh. Wash the parsley, shake dry and chop the leaves. In the oil left in the pan, toss the onions and meat over high heat until browned. Add the aubergine flesh, and remove from the heat. Stir in the tomatoes and tomato purée.

3 Return to the stove and cook over medium heat for about 5 minutes.

Season with salt and pepper. Stir the parsley, breadcrumbs and half the cheese into the meat mixture. Brush a large baking sheet with a little oil, arrange the aubergine shells on it, side by side, and fill with the meat mixture.

4 Preheat the oven to 220°C (425°F or Mark 7). In a small saucepan, heat the butter. Stir in the flour and cook until lightly browned. Stir in the milk and bring to the boil. Simmer over low heat for 5 to 8 minutes, stirring constantly, until the sauce thickens. Remove from the heat and season with salt and pepper, lemon juice and nutmeg. Whisk the egg and stir into the sauce with the rest of the cheese. Pour a thick layer of sauce over the aubergines, and bake in the centre of the oven for about 30 minutes. Serve hot.

MEAT

In Greece, as in other countries where much of the landscape is not well suited to large-scale dairy farming, meat is particularly prized. It appears mainly in the form of lamb and goat from small flocks. Veal, chicken and rabbit are also popular, and there is a wide variety of dishes made from minced lamb or beef.

Because meat is such a treat, the Greeks traditionally eat less during the week, combining it with vegetables in hearty hotpots or minced in pasta dishes; lavish meat stews and large roasts are saved for Sundays and feast days. Lamb and kid, for example, are traditional fare for Easter Sunday, when picnickers spit-roast them out of doors over glowing charcoal. Smoke curls up into the clear blue sky from among the olive trees, heavy with the aroma of sizzling meat and sweet-scented herbs.

Almost every part of an animal provides the basis for some dish. The Greeks' love of offal includes not only liver, kidneys and heart, but also extends to ram's testicles and lamb's intestines, which are chopped into small pieces, tied into knots and cooked with onions. Because some of these dishes may be too exotic for the tastes of many western Europeans, and the ingredients are not always available, they do not appear in this book. Even without them, the range of mouth-watering meat recipes is wide.

Stifado

Braised veal

Takes time • Central Greece

Serves 4

800 g shoulder or neck of veal
37.5 cl red wine
2 bay leaves
5 cm piece cinnamon stick
2 cloves
800 g shallots
4 garlic cloves
300 g beef tomatoes
6 tbsp olive oil
½ tsp sugar
salt
freshly ground black pepper

Preparation time: 2 hours
(plus 12 hours' marinating time)

1,900 kJ/450 calories per portion

1 Wash the veal, pat dry and cut into 5 cm cubes. Place in a bowl and pour over the wine. Add the bay leaves, cinnamon and cloves. Refrigerate to marinate overnight.

2 When you are ready to cook, peel the shallots and garlic. Plunge the tomatoes into boiling water, skin them and dice the flesh. Drain the meat, reserving the wine and spices.

3 Heat the oil in a large heavy pan or fireproof casserole over medium heat. Fry the meat, in batches if necessary, until browned all over, then remove from the pan. In the fat and meat juices left in the pan, sauté the shallots and garlic until transparent. Stir in the tomatoes and braise for 2 to 3 minutes more.

4 Return the meat to the pan. Add the wine and spices, and season with a little sugar and salt, and plenty of pepper. Cover and cook over low heat for 1 to 1¼ hours, until the meat is tender. Stir occasionally, taking care not to break up the shallots. If the liquid evaporates too fast, add a little water. Check seasoning and serve.

Note: Hare or rabbit also taste good prepared in this way.

Wine: A red Archanes from Crete goes well with *Stifado*.

Keftedes me salsa domates

Meatballs in tomato sauce

Fairly easy • Athens

Serves 4

400 g ripe tomatoes
5 tbsp olive oil • salt
freshly ground black pepper
½ tsp sugar • ½ tsp hot paprika
3 tbsp red wine
1 small sprig fresh thyme
500 g minced beef
1 stale bread roll
1 onion • 1 garlic clove
15 g flat-leaf parsley
9 fresh mint leaves or ½ tsp
dried mint
1 egg
1 tbsp ouzo (or a little lemon juice)
1 tbsp flour

Preparation time: 45 minutes

1,700 kJ/400 calories per portion

1 Plunge the tomatoes briefly into boiling water, skin and halve. Dice the flesh. In a large pan, heat 2 tbsp of the olive oil and braise the tomatoes briefly over medium heat. Stir in a little salt and pepper, the sugar, paprika and red wine. Cover, and simmer over low heat for about 15 minutes. Wash the thyme, shake dry and chop the leaves.

2 Put the meat in a mixing bowl. Soak the bread in water. Peel and finely chop the onion and garlic; mix with the meat. Wash and chop the parsley and fresh mint, if using. Add the parsley and fresh or dried mint to the meat. Squeeze the bread dry, break it up and stir into the meat with the egg, ouzo and some salt and pepper. Knead well.

3 Shape into little balls—about 1 heaped tbsp per ball. Put the flour on a plate and coat the meatballs in it. Heat the remaining oil in a frying pan and fry the meatballs until brown all over.

4 Check the tomato sauce, adding a little water if it seems too thick. Bring to the boil and stir in the thyme. Add the meatballs and simmer for 8 to 10 minutes. Serve with crusty bread.

Variation: Smyrna sausages
For *Souzoukakia smyrnaika*, omit the mint and ouzo, but add 1 to 2 tsp ground cumin and 1 to 2 tbsp wine to the meat mixture. Shape into small cigar-shaped sausages, coat in flour and fry as above, then add to the sauce.

Arni sto fourno

Not difficult • Peloponnese

Roast lamb

Serves 4 to 5

1 leg of lamb (about 1.5 kg)
juice of 1½ lemons
salt
freshly ground black pepper
1 small sprig fresh rosemary
4 garlic cloves
1 kg waxy potatoes
6 tbsp olive oil, or 75 g melted butter
2 sprigs fresh, or 1 tsp dried, thyme
2 sprigs fresh, or 1 tsp dried, mint

Preparation time: 2½ hours

3,100 kJ/740 calories per portion (if serving 5)

1 Trim the fat from the lamb, leaving only a thin layer. Wash the meat under cold, running water and pat dry. Place in a roasting pan, brush all over with lemon juice and season lightly with salt and pepper. Wash the rosemary, shake dry and place under the joint.

2 Preheat the oven to 180°C (350°F or Mark 4). Peel and slice the garlic, and cut into thin matchsticks. Make slits in the meat with the point of a sharp knife and insert the garlic.

3 Peel and wash the potatoes. Cut in half lengthwise and arrange round the lamb. Sprinkle the meat with a little salt and pepper and the rest of the lemon juice. Pour the oil or butter over the meat and potatoes, and add 1 cup hot water to the pan.

4 Place the pan in the centre of the oven and roast for about 1 hour, basting from time to time with the pan juices. If the juices begin to dry, add a little more hot water.

5 Turn the meat and potatoes, then roast for 1 hour more. Meanwhile, if using fresh thyme and mint, wash, shake dry and chop the leaves. About 10 minutes before the end of the cooking time, sprinkle the fresh or dried herbs over the meat and potatoes. Serve hot, accompanied by spinach or green beans sautéed in butter.

Wine: This dish goes well with a red Mavro wine from Nemea in the Peloponnese.

Kotopoulo me bamies

Chicken with okra

Fairly easy • Central Greece **Serves 4**

1 oven-ready roasting chicken
(about 1.2 kg)
salt
freshly ground black pepper
100 g spring onions
400 g tomatoes
600 g okra, preferably small
2 tbsp wine vinegar
4 tbsp olive oil
12.5 cl dry white wine

Preparation time: 1½ hours

2,300 kJ/550 calories per portion

1 Wash the chicken inside and out under cold running water. Pat dry and cut into eight pieces. Rub the pieces with a little salt and pepper.

2 Trim the spring onions. Wash under running water, shake dry and cut into short pieces. Plunge the tomatoes briefly in boiling water; core, skin and dice them. Trim the okra, taking care not to damage the pods. Place the okra in a bowl with the wine vinegar and enough cold water to cover.

3 In a large, deep frying pan, heat the olive oil until very hot. In batches if necessary, fry the chicken pieces until golden-brown all over, then remove from the oil. Fry the onions in the pan

until transparent. Add the tomatoes and fry for 30 seconds more. Stir in the wine and 25 cl water, and bring to the boil. Season with salt and pepper and add the chicken. Cover the pan and cook over medium heat for about 20 minutes. If the liquid evaporates too quickly, add another 12.5 cl hot water.

4 Drain the okra and carefully add them to the pan.

5 Continue to cook over low heat for another 20 minutes, gently shaking the pan from time to time. Do not stir; if you do, the sauce will become slimy. Serve hot, accompanied by fresh, crusty bread.

Kotopoulo me elies

Not difficult • Peloponnese   **Chicken with olives**   *Serves 4*

1 oven-ready roasting chicken
(about 1.2 kg)
600 g sweet red peppers
200 g onions • 2 garlic cloves
200 g tomatoes
100 g black olives
6 tbsp olive oil
12.5 cl red wine
3 sprigs fresh thyme • salt
freshly ground black pepper

Preparation time: 1¼ hours

2,800 kJ/670 calories per portion

1 Wash the chicken inside and out under running water, pat dry, and cut into portions. Wash and halve the sweet peppers, remove the seeds and white ribs, and cut the flesh into large pieces. Peel and finely dice the onions and garlic. Plunge the tomatoes in boiling water, skin them and dice the flesh. Drain the olives.

2 Heat the oil in a large fireproof casserole or heavy pan over high heat. Add the chicken and fry until browned all over, then remove. Add the peppers,

onions and garlic to the pan and fry over medium heat for about 2 minutes. Add the tomatoes and olives and cook for a further minute.

3 Stir in the wine, 12.5 cl water, the thyme, some salt, and a generous amount of pepper. Add the chicken and cook, covered, over low heat for about 45 minutes. Adjust the seasoning and serve with rice or fresh, crusty bread.

Wine: A red Demestica goes well with this dish.

Olives

Silvery-leaved olive trees are a common sight on slopes throughout Greece, and for many centuries their fruit has been a characteristic ingredient of the cuisine. They are eaten as a snack to accompany ouzo or wine and as a garnish for salads, and they are cooked in a wide variety of dishes; they also provide the ubiquitous olive oil for cooking and salad dressings.

The harvest begins in autumn, when the fruit is still green and unripe; later, in winter, half-ripe purple olives and ripe black olives are collected. The market stalls and the *lathatika*, or olive shop, offer a range of varieties from different regions. Attica is the home

of *tsakistes*, crushed green olives preserved in brine and herbs. Unusually large olives are found at Amfissa, near the Gulf of Corinth, and at Agrinio, not far from the Ionian coast. The finest black olives come from Arahova on Mount Parnassus and Kalamata in the Peloponnese, while the islands of Samos and Crete provide ripe, wrinkled olives called *throumbes*.

In rural areas, many people still

preserve their own olives. The fruit—bitter and inedible unless treated—is soaked in water for three to four days, the water being changed each day. Then salt is added—enough to float a fresh egg—and the olives are pickled for four to six weeks, the water being changed weekly. Finally, the olives are pickled in a mixture of olive oil, lemon juice, thyme and garlic.

Moscari me kidonia

Veal with quinces

Needs a little care • Dodecanese

Serves 4

800 g slightly streaky veal
1 medium-sized onion
800 g ripe quinces
6 tbsp olive oil
1 scant tbsp sugar
1 small cinnamon stick
ground cumin
salt
freshly ground black pepper
10 cl orange juice
small piece of rind from an
unwaxed orange
1 sprig fresh mint

Preparation time: 1 to 1¼ hours

1,700 kJ/400 calories per portion

1 Wash the meat under cold, running water, pat dry and cut into 3 cm cubes. Peel the onion and cut into small dice. Peel and core the quinces and cut the flesh into small pieces.

2 Heat half the olive oil in a fireproof casserole or heavy pan. Add the quinces, sprinkle the sugar over them, then cook over high heat, stirring constantly, until the quinces are lightly caramelized. Add 30 cl water, bring to the boil, then remove from the heat.

3 In another pan, heat the remaining oil. Add the meat and onion, and fry over high heat until browned all over. Stir in the cinnamon, a little cumin and salt, and a generous amount of pepper, and cook briefly.

4 Add the orange juice to the meat and bring to the boil. Transfer to the casserole with the quinces and stir. Cover, and cook over low heat for 30 to 40 minutes, adding a little more water if the liquid evaporates too quickly.

5 Meanwhile, finely shred the orange rind. Wash the mint leaves under running water and shake dry. Check the meat for seasoning, and garnish with orange rind and mint. Serve with rice or fresh, crusty bread.

Wine: A medium-dry white wine from Crete goes well with this dish.

Note: Chicken, pork or lamb also taste delicious cooked with quinces.

Hirino me selino

Pork ragout with celeriac

Fairly easy • Central Greece

Serves 4

200 g onions
800 g diced pork
30 g parsley
40 g clarified butter
25 cl dry white wine
salt
freshly ground black pepper
700 g celeriac, preferably small
bulbs
2 eggs
juice of 1 lemon

Preparation time: 1¾ hours

3,200 kJ/760 calories per portion

1 Peel and dice the onions. Wash the meat under cold, running water and pat dry. Wash the parsley, shake dry and chop the leaves.

2 Heat the butter in a large heavy pan over high heat. Add the meat and fry until it has browned all over and the meat juices have evaporated. Add the onions and fry until transparent.

3 Stir the wine, parsley and 37.5 cl hot water into the meat, and bring to the boil. Season with salt and pepper, cover and cook over low heat for about 45 minutes.

4 Meanwhile, peel the celeriac and cut it into medium-sized cubes. After 45 minutes' cooking, stir them into the meat. Add 12.5 cl hot water, cover and continue to cook for about 30 minutes more. Remove from the heat. In a bowl, whisk together the eggs and the lemon juice, and stir in 4 to 5 tbsp of the sauce from the pan. Stir the mixture into the meat and heat through, without boiling, stirring constantly. Serve with fresh, crusty bread.

Wine: A dry white Kouros, a country wine from Attica, is an ideal accompaniment to this ragout.

Hirino me gigantes

Not difficult • Many regions

Pork and beans

Serves 4

*250 g large dried haricot beans or
butter beans*
600 g slightly streaky leg of pork
1 medium-sized onion
300 g tomatoes
*2 sprigs fresh thyme, or 1 tsp
dried thyme*
30 g butter
1 tbsp tomato purée
salt
freshly ground black pepper
30 g flat-leaf parsley

*Preparation time: about 2 hours
(plus 8 hours' soaking time)*

2,800 kJ/670 calories per portion

1 Soak the beans in 1 litre water for 8 hours or overnight.

2 Drain the beans. Place in a pan with enough fresh cold water to cover, then bring to the boil without covering the pan. Boil briskly for a few minutes, skim off the scum, cover and simmer over low heat for about 45 minutes.

3 Meanwhile, wash the pork under cold, running water, pat dry and cut into 3 to 4 cm cubes. Peel and finely dice the onion. Plunge the tomatoes briefly in boiling water, skin them and dice the flesh. If using fresh thyme, wash, shake dry and tear off the leaves.

4 Heat the butter In a fireproof casserole until it foams. Add the meat and fry over high heat until browned all over. Reduce the heat to medium, add the onion and fry until transparent. Stir in the tomatoes and cook for 30 seconds more. Mix the tomato purée with 37.5 cl water and stir in. Season with salt, a generous amount of pepper and the thyme, and cook over low heat for 20 minutes.

5 Drain the beans and stir into the meat. Continue to cook for 30 to 45 minutes more. About 10 minutes before the end of the cooking time, wash the parsley under running water, chop the leaves and stir into the meat. Adjust the seasoning, and serve with fresh wholemeal bread.

Herbs

For thousands of years, the Greeks have used herbs widely, not just for seasoning food but for medicines too. Indeed, more of the countless herbs that grow in the wild are valued for their medical properties than are used in cookery. Basil, for example, is made into an infusion to relieve stomach ache whilst, grown in window boxes and on balconies, its scent keeps the flies away.

Of those herbs used for cooking, the most popular are oregano and thyme, which grow practically everywhere, scenting the wind with their perfume. Flat-leaf parsley and dill are added to many dishes as they cook, or at the last minute. Mint is an essential ingredient in rice and

cheese recipes, whilst rosemary seasons baked and grilled dishes, and the delicate flavour of celery and fennel leaves complements fish. Bay leaves—often from bushes the Greeks cultivate in their gardens—are an indispensable seasoning for both fish and meat.

Over their long history, herbs have acquired their own rituals and stories.

According to legend, the Virgin Mary spread her cloak to dry over a patch of rosemary, turning the flowers sky-blue. In church, the priest dips basil in holy water to bless it. In antiquity, it was usual to burn bay leaves while consulting the oracle, and the warriors of Homer's *Iliad* fed their horses parsley as a special reward.

Kouneli me kamaki

Rabbit in cream sauce

Fairly easy • Northern Greece

Serves 4

1 oven-ready rabbit (about 1.8 kg)
cut into pieces
50 cl medium-dry white wine
1 medium-sized onion
40 g clarified butter • salt
freshly ground black pepper
2 bay leaves • 2 cloves
200 g crème fraîche
30 g flat-leaf parsley

Preparation time: 1½ hours
(plus 12 hours' marinating time)

3,700 kJ/880 calories per portion

1 Wash the rabbit pieces under cold, running water, pat dry and place them in a bowl. Pour the wine over and cover, then leave in a cool place to marinate overnight.

2 When you are ready to cook, peel and dice the onion. Drain the rabbit, reserving the wine, and pat dry. Heat the clarified butter in a heavy pan or fireproof casserole and fry the rabbit over medium heat until lightly browned all over. Sprinkle with salt and pepper and transfer to a plate.

3 In the fat remaining in the pan, fry the onion until transparent. Stir in the reserved wine and a little salt. Add the rabbit pieces, cover and cook over low heat for about 30 minutes.

4 Add the bay leaves and cloves, and slowly stir in the crème fraîche. Continue to cook over low heat for a further 20 minutes. Meanwhile, wash the parsley, shake dry and chop the leaves. Check the rabbit for seasoning and sprinkle over the parsley. Serve with pasta or rice.

Bifteki me tiri

Beefburgers with feta cheese

Quick and easy • Northern Greece

Serves 4

500 g lean minced beef
1 medium-sized onion
30 g flat-leaf parsley
1 tsp dried oregano
½ tsp paprika
½ tsp cumin
salt
2 slices day-old bread
2 eggs
150 g feta cheese
6 tbsp olive oil

Preparation time: 45 minutes

2,100 kJ/500 calories per portion

1 Place the meat in a bowl. Peel and finely dice the onion, and add to the meat. Rinse the parsley under running water and shake dry. Reserve half the leaves, finely chop the rest and stir into the meat with the oregano, paprika, cumin and some salt.

2 Soak the bread in water and squeeze out any excess liquid. Break the eggs and stir into the meat with the bread. Knead the mixture until smooth, then divide into eight portions. Rinse a soup dish in cold water. One at a time, place the meat portions in the hollow of the plate and press into flat cakes.

3 Place an eighth of the feta cheese in the middle of one half of each beefburger, fold over the other half and press down firmly to seal the edges, so that the cheese does not leak out during frying.

4 In a large frying pan, heat the olive oil. In batches if necessary, fry the beefburgers over fairly high heat for about 2 minutes on each side, until they feel firm when pressed with a spatula. Serve garnished with the reserved parsley.

Wine: Choose a red Kouros or retsina.

Katsikzaki che chimo porotkali

A little more complex • Crete   **Kid in orange juice**   *Serves 4*

1 kg leg of kid
37.5 cl freshly squeezed
orange juice
3 strips unwaxed orange rind, about
4 cm long
juice of ½ lemon • 2 garlic cloves
4 sprigs fresh thyme • 200 g shallots
40 g clarified butter
¼ tsp sugar • salt
freshly ground black pepper
3 tbsp brandy
250 g hylopittes, or ribbon-shaped
pasta such as tagliatelli
70 g grated kefalograviera cheese

Preparation time: 1¼ hours
(plus 12 hours' marinating time)

3,400 kJ/810 calories per portion

1 Wash the meat under running water, pat dry and cut into 3 cm cubes. Place in a bowl and add the orange juice, rind and lemon juice. Peel and halve the garlic and add to the bowl with the thyme. Cover and refrigerate for at least 12 hours, or overnight.

2 Preheat the oven to 200°C (400°F or Mark 6). Peel the shallots and halve or quarter lengthwise. Drain the meat, reserving the marinade. Extract and reserve the orange rind, garlic and thyme. Heat the butter in a fireproof casserole and fry the meat over low heat until it is browned all over and the juices have evaporated. Stir in the garlic and shallots; fry until transparent.

3 Add the reserved marinade and 50 cl water, and bring to the boil. Stir in the orange rind, thyme and sugar, and season with salt and pepper. Cover and cook in the centre of the oven for about 15 minutes. Reduce the oven temperature to 180°C (350°F or Mark 4), and continue to cook for a further 15 minutes.

4 Stir in 50 cl hot water and the brandy. Season with salt and pepper. Stir in the pasta, cover and bake for a further 15 to 20 minutes, stirring once. Sprinkle with the grated cheese, and serve at once, accompanied by fresh, crusty bread.

Bread

The usual accompaniment to every Greek meal is bread, which often still comes from the traditional dome-shaped clay ovens of village bakeries (*right*). It appears in many forms, the most common of which include *fratzola*, a long, crusty white loaf, and *karveli*, which is made from a blend of different flours and baked in oval or round loaves. *Paximadia*, twice-baked, dry bread, is available everywhere.

Bread is more than a staple, however, and the normal variety is surpassed by the many special breads produced to celebrate feast days. Christmas, for example, is marked with *christopsomo*, while a

week later *vasilopitta* is baked to see in the New Year. At the beginning of Lent, 40 days before Easter, bakers produce *lagana*: a flat, oval, unleavened loaf that is sprinkled with sesame seeds. *Lazarapso*, made with currants and sesame seeds, is enjoyed on Easter Saturday, while the traditional

Easter Day bread is *tsourekia*.

To mark religious festivals in general, *prosforo*, or church bread, is blessed by the priest and taken home by the congregation, whilst on Crete, bread decorated with flowers is used to celebrate weddings, with guests keeping pieces as souvenirs.

Souvlakia arniou

Quick and easy • Many regions

Lamb kebabs

Serves 4

800 g leg of lamb
8 bay leaves • 12.5 cl olive oil
juice of 1 lemon
12.5 cl dry white wine
2 tsp dried oregano
salt • freshly ground black pepper
250 g shallots

*Preparation time: 30 minutes
(plus 12 hours'
marinating time)*

*3,200 kJ/760 calories
per portion*

1 Rinse the meat under cold, running water, pat dry and cut into 3 cm cubes. Halve the bay leaves. In a bowl, mix the olive oil with the lemon juice, wine, bay leaves and oregano, and season with salt and pepper. Stir in the meat to coat thoroughly. Cover and refrigerate for at least 12 hours, or overnight.

2 When you are ready to cook, peel the shallots. Drain the meat, then thread the meat, shallots and halved bay leaves alternately onto long wooden skewers, pressing them tightly together.

3 Place the kebabs under a hot grill and cook for about 4 to 5 minutes on each side, depending on the thickness of the meat, until the lamb is browned and tender. Serve with boiled rice.

Wine: A potent red *vin ordinaire* or retsina goes well with lamb kebabs.

Note: If you like, add diced tomatoes or strips of sweet pepper to the kebabs before grilling.

Arni me anginares

Lamb with artichokes

Serves 4

8 small artichokes (about 1 kg)
juice of 1½ lemons
700 g leg of lamb
1 medium-sized onion
15 g parsley
15 g dill
40 g butter
1 scant tbsp flour
salt
freshly ground black pepper
2 eggs

Preparation time: 2 hours

2,600 kJ/620 calories
per portion

1 Pull off the tough outer leaves of the artichokes and, with scissors, trim the tips of the rest. Trim the stalks and peel thinly. Halve the artichokes lengthwise and remove the purple leaves and hairy chokes. Immediately place the artichokes in a bowl of cold water mixed with 6 tbsp of the lemon juice.

2 Wash the meat under cold, running water, pat dry, and cut into 3 cm cubes. Peel and finely dice the onion. Wash the parsley and dill, shake dry, and finely chop the leaves. In a large heavy pan, heat the butter and brown the meat over medium heat. Add the onion and fry briefly until transparent.

3 Stir the flour into the pan and add just enough water to cover the meat.

Bring to the boil, stirring constantly. Season with salt, pepper and 2 tbsp of the lemon juice. Stir in half the chopped herbs.

4 Arrange the artichokes on top of the meat, cover, and continue to cook for 45 minutes to 1 hour, until the meat and artichokes are tender. If necessary, add a little hot water.

5 In a bowl, whisk the eggs and the remaining lemon juice. Allow the meat to cool slightly. Whisk a little of the meat sauce into the eggs, then stir into the meat. Heat through without boiling. Sprinkle with the remaining chopped herbs, and serve.

Wine: A dry, white St Helena from the Peloponnese goes well with this dish.

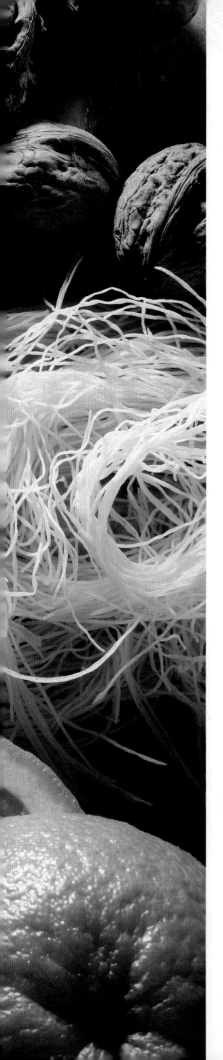

CAKES AND PASTRIES

Although some tourist hotels have introduced desserts to satisfy foreign visitors who are used to a sweet dish at the end of the menu, the traditional Greek meal usually ends with an attractively presented dish of fruits in season, followed by a cup of strong coffee.

However, the Greeks have a very sweet tooth and cakes, pastries and other sweetmeats are always available. Pastry shops, or *zacharoplasteia*, abound, and every household keeps a supply of sugary titbits to eat between meals or as a late evening snack. Like their Middle Eastern neighbours, the Greeks are fond of sweets and pastries soaked in sugar or honey syrup.

Greek people are very hospitable. When families have guests, or friends drop in unexpectedly, they are usually welcomed with something sweet to eat: biscuits or a piece of cake, or a "spoon sweet", such as sour cherries in syrup, which are always kept in the larder and traditionally served in a *glykothiki*, an egg-shaped cup from which hang several little round spoons.

Cakes and pastries are baked for family celebrations and the various religious festivals. Everyone looks forward to *kourabiedes*, the orange or rose-flavoured Christmas biscuits, and the New Year bread in which the cook hides a lucky coin. At Easter there is a special bread with red-coloured eggs baked in the dough.

Kalizunia
Cream cheese pastries

Takes time · Crete

Makes about 40 pastries

3 eggs
6 tbsp olive oil
125 g sugar
100 g yogurt
500 g plain flour
salt
1½ tsp baking powder
1 egg yolk
100 g sesame seeds

For the filling:
700 g unsalted cream cheese (for
example, ricotta)
150 g sugar · 2 tbsp honey
1 scant tbsp cinnamon

*Preparation time: 2¼ hours
(plus 1 hour's standing time)*

530 kJ/130 calories per pastry

1 With an egg whisk or hand-held electric mixer, thoroughly whisk the eggs, oil, sugar and yogurt. Stir in some of the flour, salt and baking powder, then knead in the remainder. Wrap the dough in foil so that it is airtight, and leave to stand for 1 hour.

2 Meanwhile, press the cream cheese for the filling through a sieve and stir until creamy. Add the sugar, honey and cinnamon and mix thoroughly. Preheat the oven to 180°C (350°F or Mark 4).

3 Cut the dough into four or five portions. Thinly roll out one portion, keeping the rest of the dough wrapped in foil so that it does not dry out. Using a glass with a rim about 10 cm in diameter, cut the dough into circles.

Place 1 tsp of filling in the centre of each circle, spreading it slightly. Fold two opposite edges of each circle over 2 cm of the filling on either side, leaving 2 cm uncovered. Fold the remaining two sides in the same way, making square parcels. Continue to make parcels with the remaining dough until you have enough to fill a large baking sheet.

4 Grease the baking sheet with a little butter and arrange the parcels about 2 cm apart. Whisk the egg yolk with 2 tbsp water. Avoiding the filling, brush the dough edges with egg and sprinkle with sesame seeds. Bake in the centre of the oven for about 30 minutes, until the pastries begin to turn golden-brown. Make and bake the rest of the pastries in the same way.

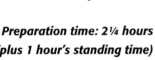

Kourabiedes
Almond biscuits

Fairly easy · Northern Greece

Makes about 40 biscuits

200 g butter
150 g sugar
1½ to 2 tsp vanilla sugar (see
Glossary)
1 tbsp ouzo
2 eggs
salt · 375 g flour
125 g ground almonds
about 40 cloves
4 tbsp rose water or orange
flower water
250 g icing sugar

*Preparation time: 1 hour
(plus 20 minutes' standing time)*

450 kJ/110 calories per biscuit

1 Melt the butter, place in a bowl or food processor with the sugar, and beat until creamy. Stir in the vanilla sugar, ouzo, eggs and a little salt. Sift the flour into the mixture. Stir in the ground almonds, then knead to a smooth dough. Cover and leave to stand in the refrigerator for about 20 minutes. Preheat the oven to 180°C (350°F or Mark 4).

2 Grease a baking sheet with a little butter. Shape the dough into a roll and break off little pieces about the size of a plum. Shape the pieces into flattish round biscuits and arrange on the baking sheet. Gently flatten the surface

with the back of a knife and place a clove in the middle of each biscuit. Bake in batches in the centre of the oven for about 20 minutes, until the biscuits are lightly browned.

3 While they are still warm, brush the biscuits with rose water or orange flower water. Put the icing sugar on a deep plate and roll the biscuits in the sugar so that they are thickly coated. Gently press the icing sugar into the biscuits, and arrange on a plate.

Note: Rose water and orange flower water are available from Greek delicatessens and specialist shops.

Diples
Lovers' knots

Fairly easy • Aegean Islands

Serves 4

4 eggs
1½ tbsp ouzo
juice of ½ lemon
½ tsp bicarbonate of soda
500 g flour
150 g sugar
3 tbsp honey
1 cinnamon stick
sunflower oil for deep frying
150 g finely chopped walnuts

Preparation time: 1¼ hours
(plus 1 hour's standing time)

3,700 kJ/880 calories per portion

1 Put the eggs, ouzo, lemon juice and bicarbonate of soda in a bowl and whisk vigorously with an egg whisk or hand-held electric beater for about 2 minutes. Add the flour, a little at a time, until the mixture is firm. Then add the remaining flour and knead the mixture to make an elastic dough. Shape the dough into a ball, wrap in foil and leave to stand in the refrigerator for about 1 hour.

2 Place the sugar, honey and cinnamon stick in a saucepan with ¾ litre water. Bring to the boil then cook over a medium heat for 7 to 8 minutes, until a thin syrup forms. Remove the pan from the heat.

3 Cut the dough into four pieces and roll each piece out very thinly. Using a fluted pastry wheel, cut the dough into rectangles, each about 6 by 3 cm. Pinch each rectangle together in the middle to make a little bow-like shape.

4 Pour a generous amount of oil into a deep frying pan and heat until small bubbles rise from a wooden spoon handle dipped into the hot oil. Deep fry the knots until golden-brown. Remove them with a slotted spoon and place briefly on a wire rack to drain, then dip them in the syrup while they are still hot. Arrange on a serving dish and serve sprinkled with chopped walnuts.

Note: Lovers' knots are a particular favourite among Greek children. They are best eaten while still warm.

Honey

Everywhere in Greece, both on the mainland and the islands, rows of pastel-coloured beehives can be seen on the hillsides, in orchards and in clearings in the pinewoods. They are a permanent feature of the Greek landscape. Each colony of bees produces its own flavour of honey, depending on the type of vegetation growing in the area.

For the dark, strongly flavoured pine honey from the heavily-wooded regions of northern and central Greece, the bees gather the protein-rich nectar of the conifers. The pale yellow honey from the nectar of lemon blossoms is also highly prized. But most popular of all—found in the Peloponnese, Crete and many of the islands—is the golden-coloured thyme honey with its delicate scent of mountain herbs.

Honey is used in a wide variety of cakes, pastries, biscuits and sweets. In Greece, where honey is often brought direct from the beekeepers, people like to eat it by the spoonful or with yogurt. Honeycomb can also be eaten; apart from honey, it contains nutritious pollen and enzymes, believed to be very effective in strengthening the immune system. The way to eat it is to bite off a piece, chew it, then spit out the wax.

Kataifi me karidia

Angel's hair rolls

500 g ready-made kataifi, or angel's hair dough
250 g finely ground walnuts or pistachios
300 g sugar
1 tsp ground cinnamon
15 cl olive oil
1 untreated lemon
2 tbsp rose water or orange flower water

Preparation time: 1¼ hours (plus 30 minutes' cooling time)

1,600 kJ/380 calories per roll

1 Remove the dough from its wrapping, lay it on a tray and cover with a damp cloth. Preheat the oven to 180°C (350°F or Mark 4). Mix 200 g of the nuts with 100 g of the sugar and the cinnamon. Grease a baking tray with a little oil.

2 Cut the skein of dough into pieces about 15 cm long, taking care that all the threads are lying in the same direction (*above*).

3 Divide each piece of the dough into strips 4 to 5 cm wide, and roughly 30 to 40 g each in weight, and lay them on a flat worktop (*above*).

4 Sprinkle the bottom end of each strip with some of the nut mixture (*above*). Starting with the nutty end, roll up a strip of angel's hair, tucking in any loose threads. Place the roll on the baking tray, with the end downwards.

5 Repeat the process with the rest of the *kataifi* dough, laying the rolls close together in the baking tray. Fill any empty space with crumpled aluminium foil. Brush the rolls generously with the olive oil, and bake in the centre of the oven until they are nicely browned, approximately 30 minutes.

6 Meanwhile, put the remaining sugar, 20 cl water, a small piece of lemon rind and the strained juice of the lemon in a saucepan and bring to the boil, stirring constantly. Continue to cook until it forms a relatively thin syrup. Allow to cool, then pour over the hot rolls. Sprinkle with rose water or orange flower water. Leave to cool for about 30 minutes, then serve, sprinkled with the rest of the nuts.

Note: *Kataifi*, or angel's hair pastry looks rather like Shredded Wheat. The dough is available ready-made from Greek or Middle Eastern food shops.

Vissino glyko

Sour cherries in syrup

Simple • Mainland Greece

Makes 4 jars

1 kg morello cherries
1 kg sugar
juice of 1 lemon

**Preparation time: 40 minutes
(plus 12 hours' standing time)**

4,700 kJ/1,100 calories per jar

1 Rinse the cherries under running water and drain. Carefully remove the stones, reserving the juice. Place alternate layers of cherries and sugar in a bowl and pour over the reserved juice. Cover and leave to stand in the refrigerator overnight to draw off the juice, then stir thoroughly.

2 Transfer the cherries and juice to a saucepan and add 10 cl water. Bring to the boil over a high heat. Strain the

lemon juice through a sieve into the pan and continue to cook, uncovered, until the syrup thickens. To test the syrup, pour a drop onto a saucer. If the syrup does not spread it is ready.

3 Using spotlessly clean, sterilized screw-top preserving jars, divide the cherries and syrup between them. Carefully wipe the rims of the jars and replace the lids firmly, then store in a cool place.

Galaktobouriko

Custard pie

More complex • Northern Greece

Makes about 30 triangles

3 eggs
300 g sugar
90 g semolina
**grated rind and juice of
1 untreated lemon**
salt
1 litre milk
**1 vanilla pod (or 2 sachets vanilla-
flavoured sugar)**
150 g butter
1 packet phyllo pastry (about 450 g)
1 cinnamon stick

Preparation time: 1¾ hours

680 kJ/160 calories per triangle

1 Break the eggs into a bowl and whisk with 200 g sugar until creamy. Gently trickle the semolina into the egg mixture, stirring constantly. Add the grated lemon rind and a pinch of salt to the egg mixture and stir in the milk. Transfer the mixture to a saucepan.

2 Scrape the seeds out of the vanilla pod, if using. Add both pod and seeds, or the vanilla-flavoured sugar, to the pan. Bring to the boil over medium heat, stirring constantly, and cook and stir until the mixture thickens. Remove from the heat, discard the pod and leave to cool, stirring from time to time.

3 Grease a large baking sheet with butter. Preheat the oven to 180°C (350°F or Mark 4). Melt the butter for brushing the pastry.

4 Unwrap the phyllo pastry. Open out the sheets and finely sprinkle with water. Cover with a damp cloth and

leave briefly. Lay half the phyllo sheets on the baking sheet, brushing each one with butter and letting the edges hang over the sides of the baking sheet. Spread the custard evenly over the top.

5 Fold the phyllo edges inwards and brush with butter. Cover with the rest of the phyllo sheets, again brushing each one with butter. Trim off the edges, or fold them under. Using a sharp knife, cut the pie into 8 by 6 cm rectangles, then make a diagonal incision across each rectangle.

6 Bake the pie in the centre of the oven for 35 to 40 minutes until lightly browned. Meanwhile, put 12.5 cl water in a saucepan, strain in the lemon juice, and add the remaining sugar and the cinnamon stick. Bring to the boil, and continue to boil briskly for 2 minutes, then remove and cool. Dribble this syrup over the hot pie. Leave to cool, then serve, cut into triangles.

Koulouria

Fairly easy • Athens **Sesame rings**

Makes 8 rings

500 g flour
1 tsp salt
3 tbsp olive oil
30 g fresh yeast (or 15 g dried yeast)
250 g sesame seeds

Preparation time: 1¼ hours
(plus 40 to 50 minutes' proving time)

1,800 kJ/430 calories per ring

1 Sift the flour into a bowl. Make a well in the middle, sprinkle the salt round the edge, then pour in the oil. Dissolve the yeast in 30 cl warm water (if using dried yeast follow packet instructions) and pour on top of the oil. Stir into a dough, then knead with your hands. The dough should be very soft. Cover with a cloth and leave to prove in a warm place for 30 to 40 minutes.

2 Preheat the oven to 220°C (425°F or Mark 7). Grease a large baking tray. Thoroughly knead the dough again, then shape it into a roll and cut into eight equal-sized pieces. Shape each piece into a thin length about 2 cm in diameter and 35 cm long. Press the ends together firmly to make a circle.

3 Fill a bowl with warm water. Pour the sesame seeds on a plate. Dip each ring briefly in the water, then dip both sides in the sesame seeds, so that they are generously coated.

4 Lay the sesame rings on the baking tray. Cover and leave to prove for a further 10 minutes, then place in the centre of the oven. After 10 minutes, sprinkle some cold water over the bottom of the oven, re-closing the door immediately, and bake for a further 15 minutes, until the rings are browned.

Karidopitta Athinaiki

Fairly easy • Athens **Athenian walnut cake**

Makes about 16 pieces

400 g shelled walnuts
8 eggs
130 g softened butter
180 g sugar
1 vanilla pod
250 g plain flour
1 tsp baking powder
grated rind of 1 untreated lemon
salt • breadcrumbs

For the syrup:
250 g sugar
juice of ½ lemon
1 cinnamon stick
1½ tbsp Greek or other brandy

Preparation time: 1¾ hours

2,400 kJ/570 calories per piece

1 Finely grind 300 g of the walnuts in a food processor, then coarsely chop the rest. Separate the eggs. Place 125 g of the butter and the sugar in a bowl or food processor. Scrape the seeds out of the vanilla pod and add to the bowl. Cream the butter and sugar until light and fluffy. Gradually beat in the egg yolks. Mix the flour and baking powder and sift into the mixture. Add the grated lemon and a pinch of salt. Stir thoroughly with a spoon.

2 Preheat the oven to 180°C (350°F or Mark 4). Beat the egg whites until stiff, then fold them into the cake mixture with the ground walnuts. Grease a 28 cm springform cake tin with the rest of the butter, sprinkle with breadcrumbs and transfer the mixture to the tin. Bake in the centre of the oven for 50 minutes to 1 hour, or until a knife inserted in the cake comes out clean.

3 To make the syrup, put the sugar, lemon juice and cinnamon stick in a saucepan with ½ litre water and cook over medium heat for up to 10 minutes—the syrup should still be quite thin. Leave to cool, discard the cinnamon stick, then stir in the brandy.

4 Pour the syrup over the hot cake in the tin, letting it soak right in. Briefly leave to stand. When cool, transfer to a serving plate and cut into square pieces. Sprinkle with the coarsely chopped walnuts before serving.

Tsourekia
Plaited Easter bread

More complex • All regions

Makes 1 loaf (about 20 slices)

scarlet egg dye (see Glossary)
few drops vinegar
8 eggs
½ tsp oil
500 g flour
40 g fresh yeast (or 20 g dried yeast)
100 g sugar
100 g butter
finely grated rind of 1 orange
½ tsp salt
1 tsp powdered aniseed
1 egg yolk
50 g sesame seeds

Preparation time: 1¾ hours (plus 1¾ hours' proving time)

860 kJ/200 calories per slice

1 Dissolve the egg dye in an old pan with a little boiling water, fill up with cold water and add the vinegar. Put 5 eggs in the pan, bring to the boil and cook for 15 minutes. Cool slightly and polish with oil so that the eggs shine.

2 Put the flour in a bowl and make a well in the middle. Mix the yeast and 1 tsp sugar with 6 tbsp warm water, and stir until smooth (if using dried yeast follow packet instructions). Pour the yeast into the well, and mix it with a little flour. Cover with a cloth and stand in a warm place for 30 minutes.

3 Warm the butter and add to the flour mixture with the grated rind, remaining sugar and 3 eggs, the salt and aniseed. Stir everything together, then knead to a dough. Cover the bowl again and leave to prove for about 1 hour in a warm place, until the dough has considerably increased in volume.

4 Preheat the oven to 180°C (350°F or Mark 4). Grease a large baking sheet. Knead the dough again. Cut off about two thirds, shape it into a loaf, about

30 cm long, and place on the baking sheet. Divide the remaining dough into four pieces. Form each piece into a strand the same length as the loaf. Twist pairs of strands together (*above*).

5 Gently press the sides of the loaf together, then wind the twisted strands round the edge (*above*) and press strands and loaf together. Whisk the egg yolk with 1 tbsp water. Brush the loaf with the egg, sprinkle generously with sesame seeds, then leave to prove for a further 15 minutes.

6 Make five round dents down the middle of the loaf, and place a coloured egg in each. Bake in the centre of the oven for 30 to 40 minutes.

Variation: New Year bread
To make *Vasilopitta*, prepare the dough as in Steps 1 to 3. Place it in a greased 28 cm diameter springform cake tin. Wrap a coin in foil and hide it in the dough. Brush with egg yolk, arrange almond halves on top in the shape of a cross and sprinkle with sesame seeds. Prove for 15 minutes, then bake as above. The bread is traditionally cut at midnight. Whoever finds the coin will have good luck in the New Year.

Suggested Menus

The Greek's great passion for food is reflected in the way that the humblest of ingredients are combined in endlessly varied and imaginative ways, creating meals to rival the most sophisticated of cuisines. This selection of menus, put together from recipes featured in the book, contains suggestions to suit every occasion, from simple, everyday meals to more elaborate or festive ones. Desserts do not feature in the majority of them as it usually just consists of fresh fruit, rounded off by a cup of strong Greek coffee and, if it is a feast day, the appropriate celebratory pastry.

Everyday menus

Peasant soup (*Soupa horiatiki*)	51
Deep-fried baby squid (*Kalamarakia tiganata*)	43
"Little shoes" (*Papoutsakia*)	104

Stuffed vegetables (*Domates ke piperies yemistes*)	97
Country salad (*Horiatiki salata*)	35
Beefburgers with feta cheese (*Bifteki me tiri*)	118
Beans in tomato sauce (*Gigantes plaki*)	28

Toasted bread with cheese, onion and tomato topping (*Dako*)	39
Lentil soup (*Soupa fakes*)	48
Lamb stew with orzo pasta (*Giouvetsi me kritharaki*)	74

Baked sardines (*Sardelles sto fourno*)	92
Wild vegetable salad (*Agriohortasalata*)	30
Meatballs in tomato sauce (*Keftedes me salsa domates*)	108

Quick menus

Fried cheese (*Saganaki*)	40
Country salad (*Horiatiki salata*)	35
Metsovo-style pasta squares (*Hylopittes metsovou*)	78

Trahana soup (*Soupa trahana*)	53
Aubergines baked with eggs (*Avga matia melitzanes*)	70
Lamb kebabs (*Souvlakia arniou*)	122

Cabbage, carrot and egg salad (*Lahanosalata me karota*)	36
Baked sweet peppers (*Piperies sto fourno*)	26
Pork and beans (*Hirino me gigantes*)	116

Courgette pie (*Kolokithobouriko*)	63
Yogurt with cucumber (*Tzatziki*)	27
Bonito with vegetables (*Palamida plaki*)	90

Menus to prepare in advance

Black-eyed pea salad (*Salata fassolia mavromatica*)	36
Stuffed vine leaves (*Dolmades*)	44
Meat pie (*Kreatopitta*)	58

Chick-pea soup (*Revithia soupa*)	50
Baked macaroni and leeks (*Pastitsio me prassa*)	76
Octopus in wine (*Oktapodi krassato*)	84

Beetroot salad (*Patsaria salata*)	34
Garlic and potato purée (*Skordalia me patates*)	43
Lamb stew with orzo pasta (*Giouvetsi me kritharaki*)	74

Spinach and rice (*Spanakorizo*)	76
Fried cheese (*Saganaki*)	40
Meat and macaroni pie (*Pastitsio*)	73

Vegetarian menus

Courgette fritters (*Kolokithakia keftedes*)	28
Yogurt with cucumber (*Tzatziki*)	27
Spinach pie (*Spanakopitta*)	56

Split pea purée (*Fava*)	39
Toasted bread with cheese, onion and tomato topping (*Dako*)	39
Vegetable bake (*Briami*)	96

Lentil soup (*Soupa fakes*)	48
Beetroot salad (*Patsaria salata*)	34
Artichokes and broad beans (*Anginares me koukia*)	98

Meat menus

Meat pie (*Kreatopitta*)	58
Country salad (*Horiatiki salata*)	35
Kid in orange juice (*Katsikzaki che chimo porotkali*)	120

Beefburgers with feta cheese (*Bifteki me tiri*)	118
Beetroot salad (*Patsaria salad*)	34
Chicken with olives (*Kotopoulo me elies*)	112

Chicken soup with egg and lemon (*Kotosoupa avgolemono*)	48
Baked sweet peppers (*Piperies sto fourno*)	26
"Little shoes" (*Papoutsakia*)	104

Yogurt with cucumber (*Tzatziki*)	27
Stuffed vine leaves (*Dolmades*)	44
Lamb kebabs (*Souvlakia arniou*)	122

Fish menus

Fish roe purée (*Taramosalata*)	33
Baked prawns (*Garides giouvetsi*)	41
Braised salt cod (*Bakaliaros yiahni*)	88

Stuffed squid (*Kalamarakia yemisto*)	91
Country salad (*Horiatiki salata*)	35
Bonito with vegetables (*Palamida plaki*)	90

Split-pea purée (*Fava*) 39
Baked peppers (*Piperies sto fourno*) 26
Marinated swordfish (*Xiphios marinatos*) 87

Spring menus

Wild vegetable omelette (*Omeletta agriohorta*) 68
Cream cheese pasties (*Mitzithropittakia*) 60
Lamb with artichokes (*Arni me anginares*) 123

Soupa horiatiki (*Peasant soup*) 51
Wild vegetable salad (*Agriohortasalata*) 30
Chicken with okra (*Kotopoulo me bamies*) 111

Summer menus

Okra in tomato sauce (*Bamies laderes*) 103
Baked sardines (*Sardelles sto fourno*) 92
Aubergines baked with meat (*Moussaka*) 100

Yogurt with cucumber (*Tzatziki*) 27
Country salad (*Horiatiki salata*) 35
Stuffed vine leaves (*Dolmades*) 44
Fish kebabs (*Souvlakia psaria*) 87

Courgette pie (*Kolokithobouriko*) 63
Fish kebabs (*Souvlakia psaria*) 87
  with Garlic and potato purée (*Skordalia me patates*) 43
Country salad (*Horiatiki salata*) 35

Courgette fritters (*Kolokithakia keftedes*) 28
Mussels with rice (*Midia me risi*) 73
Artichoke and spinach bake (*Anginares me spanaki*) 98

Autumn menus

Aubergines baked with eggs (*Avga matia melitzanes*) 70
Beetroot salad (*Patsaria salata*) 34
Bonito with vegetables (*Palamida plaki*) 90

Baked sweet peppers (*Piperies sto fourno*) 26
Stuffed squid (*Kalamarakia yemisto*) 91
Baked macaroni and leeks (*Pastitsio me prassa*) 76

Chick-pea soup (*Revithia soupa*) 50
Spinach pie (*Spanakopitta*) 56
Chicken with olives (*Kotopoulo me elies*) 112

Winter menus

Lentil soup (*Soupa fakes*) 48
Deep-fried mussels (*Midia tiganita*) 33
Braised veal (*Stifado*) 108

Beans in tomato sauce (*Gigantes plaki*) 28
Cabbage, carrot & egg salad (*Lachanosalata me karota*) 36
Veal with quinces (*Moscari me kidonia*) 115

Trahana soup (*Soupa trahana*) 53
Black-eyed pea salad (*Salata fassolia mavromatica*) 36
Pork ragout with celeriac (*Hirino me selino*) 115

Dinner party menus

Fish roe purée (*Taramosalata*) 33
Baked sweet peppers (*Piperies sto fourno*) 26
Yogurt with cucumber (*Tzatziki*) 27
Country salad (*Horiatiki salata*) 35
Deep-fried mussels (*Midia tiganita*) 33
Garlic and potato purée (*Skordalia me patates*) 43
Black-eyed pea salad (*Salata fassolia mavromatica*) 36
Aubergines baked with meat (*Moussaka*) 100
Angel's hair rolls (*Kataifi me karidia*) 130

Cream cheese pasties (*Mitzithropittakia*) 60
Stuffed vine leaves (*Dolmades*) 44
Yogurt with cucumber (*Tzatziki*) 27
Meatballs in tomato sauce (*Keftedes me salsa domates*) 108
Baked sea bream (*Lithrini fourno ala spetsiota*) 82
Marinated swordfish (*Xiphios marinatos*) 87
Athenian walnut cake (*Karidopitta Athinaiki*) 135

Festive menus

Easter
Cheese triangles (*Tiropittakia*) 64
Courgette fritters (*Kolokithakia keftedes*) 28
Wild vegetable salad (*Agriohortasalata*) 30
Roast lamb (*Arni sto fourno*) 110
Plaited Easter bread (*Tsourekia*) 136

Christmas
Chicken soup with egg and lemon (*Kotosoupa avgolemono*) 48
Baked prawns (*Garides giouvetsi*) 41
Cabbage, carrot and egg salad (*Lachanosalata me karota*) 36
Meat and macaroni pie (*Pastitsio*) 73
Chicken with olives (*Kotopoulo me elies*) 112
  or Rabbit in cream sauce (*Kouneli me kamaki*) 118
Almond biscuits (*Kourabiedes*) 126

New Year's Eve
Deep-fried baby squid (*Kalamarakia tiganita*) 43
Garlic and potato purée (*Skordalia me patates*) 43
Fish roe purée (*Taramosalata*) 33
Beetroot salad (*Patsaria salata*) 34
Braised veal (*Stifado*) 108
New Year bread (*Vasilopitta*) 136
Lovers' knots (*Diples*) 128

Glossary

This Glossary is intended as a brief guide to some less familiar cookery terms and ingredients, including Greek words or items found on menus.

Agriodiosmos: mint. The fresh or dried leaves are used to season rice and cheese fillings for pies and pastries.

Agriohorta: wild spring vegetables such as young dandelion leaves, nettle tips, watercress and spinach. They are used in salads and cooked dishes.

al dente: literally "to the tooth". The ideal consistency for cooked pasta, vegetables and rice, tender but still firm to the bite.

Anithos: dill. The fresh herb is used extensively in Greece for seasoning vegetables, fish, rice dishes and pie fillings.

Arni: lamb

Athotiros: a mild-tasting cheese from the island of Crete

Attica: a wine-growing region in central Greece. It is the main source of retsina.

Avgo: egg

Avgolemono: a method of binding and seasoning soups and sauces with beaten egg and lemon juice.

Baklava: a rich sweetmeat made from sheets of phyllo pastry interlaced with walnuts, almonds and honey.

Baste: to pour or spoon oil fat or liquid over food to prevent it from drying during cooking.

Black-eyed peas: small, creamy-coloured beans with a black "spot" where they were joined to the pod.

Blanch: to plunge food into boiling water for a short period. It is done for a number of reasons: to facilitate skinning foods such as tomatoes; to remove strong flavours; or to soften vegetables before cooking.

Bonito: a meaty-fleshed Mediterranean fish belonging to the mackerel family.

Chick-peas: small, pale-golden hard peas resembling hazelnuts. Their nutty flavour enhances stews and casseroles, and is an essential ingredient in the Greek dip *hummus.*

Chili peppers: a variety of hot red or green peppers. They contain volatile oils that can irritate the skin and eyes and must be handled with caution. Wash hands immediately after using them.

Clarified butter: butter from which the water, milk solids and salt have been removed, so that it can be used for cooking at higher temperatures. You can make it at home by gently heating butter up to boiling point, then allowing it to separate and straining off the pure melted butter.

Daphne: bay tree. Trees and bushes of this evergreen plant flourish throughout Greece. The leaves feature widely in the cuisine, in roasts, sauces and stews. They are also good for flavouring fish stock.

Demestica: a popular dry, light, inexpensive table wine.

Dentrolivano: rosemary, which grows profusely in Greece. Sprigs or leaves are used fresh or dried for seasoning roasts and grills.

Dolmades: stuffed vine leaves—a typically Greek dish

Elies: olives

Estiatorio: a restaurant; more formal than a taverna.

Feta: a soft, rindless, salty cheese made from ewe's or goat's milk and preserved in brine. It is best to rinse it before use to get rid of the excessive saltiness.

Fraoula: a strawberry liqueur from the island of Zakynthos

Garides: prawns

Glyka: fruit preserves traditionally offered to guests, and eaten on festive occasions. Also known as "spoon sweets".

Goumenissa: a wine-growing region of western Macedonia

Greek salad: starter or main course dish traditionally comprising tomatoes, cucumber, feta cheese and black olives

Haloumi: a semi-hard, creamy cheese with a salty taste. It is used for cooking.

Halva: a rich sweetmeat made from, among other ingredients, nuts, sesame seeds, semolina, olive oil and sugar

Horiatiko: an off-white country bread, made in flat loaves

Hylopittes: small, square-shaped pasta

Kafeneon: a coffee house

Kafes: coffee. The traditional thick Greek brew is called *elenikos* and is served with the grounds from a long-handled copper or aluminium pot.

Kalamata: a region of the Peloponnese, famous for its large, oblong olives.

Kasseri: a hard, mild ewe's milk cheese. It is used in cooking.

Kataifi (also known as angel's hair pastry): fine threads of pastry resembling Shredded Wheat. It is available fresh or dried from specialist Greek delicatessens.

Kefalograviera (also shortened just to *graviera*): a rich, creamy cheese made from ewe's or goat's milk. It is similar to Gruyère.

Kefalotyri: a hard, tangy grating cheese made from ewe's or goat's milk, sold at varying degrees of maturity. It has a fat content of between 40 and 50 per cent.

Keftedes: minced meatballs—a popular Greek dish

Kidonopasto: quince paste, a speciality of the Ionian islands.

Kitron: a lemon liqueur from Naxos

Kotopoulo: chicken

Koulouria: rings of white bread sprinkled with sesame seeds

Krasi: wine

Kritharaki (also known as orzo): pasta shaped like grains of rice. It is used in soups and stews.

Lathatika: olive shop

Limnos: northern Aegean island producing a sweet golden Muscat wine

Loukanika: spicy sausage

Loukoumades: hot cinnamon and honey fritters

Maidanos: flat-leaf parsley. It grows all year round in Greece and has a slightly milder flavour than the more familiar crinkly variety.

Malvasia: a famous Greek grape variety

Manouri: a lightly salted soft cheese from the island of Crete

Mantinia: a high-altitude wine-growing region in the Peloponnese. It produces dry, fruity white wines.

Mantzourana: majoram. It is used fresh or dried in the same way as oregano.

Marathos: fennel. The feathery leaves and dried seeds of the herb (also known as wild fennel) have a mild anise flavour. Its vegetable relative (also known as finocchio) can be cooked, or eaten raw in salads.

Marinade: a seasoning mixture to coat or soak meat or fish before cooking in order to tenderize or impart flavour. A wet marinade is usually made from oil, herbs, vegetables and seasoning mixed with wine, vinegar or lemon juice; a dry marinade consists of a mixture of salt, herbs and spices.

Mavro: the general word for red wines; it literally translates as "black".

Mavrodaphne: a heavy, sweet ruby-red dessert wine

Mayiritsa: a soup made from the offal of the young spring lamb. It is traditionally served on Easter Saturday night.

Melitzanes: aubergines. One of the most commonly used vegetables in Greece, an essential ingredient in *moussaka*.

Menta: peppermint

Metaxa: Greek brandy

Mezedes: small hot or cold appetizers

Midia: mussels

Mitzithra: a semi-soft cream cheese similar to ricotta, usually made from ewe's milk. It is used unsalted for desserts, and salted for savoury pies.

Moussaka: a traditional Greek dish comprising layers of sliced aubergine, minced lamb and bechamel sauce

Naoussa: a famous wine-growing region of Macedonia. It produces strong dry red wines.

Nemea: town in the eastern Peloponnese. The dry, full-bodied red wine of the region is known as "lion's blood".

Nero: water

Okra (also known as lady's fingers): a vegetable cultivated widely in northern Greece

Orange flower water: a fragrant liquid derived from the essential oil distilled from orange blossom. It is used to perfume and flavour confectionery.

Ouzeria: a small bar principally serving ouzo (*see below*), often accompanied by *mezedes*, or small appetizers

Ouzo: a strong, clear spirit distilled from the remains of the grapes after pressing (in some Arab countries it is distilled from figs). It has a distinctive aniseed flavour and high alcohol content. It is drunk throughout Greece, often mixed with chilled water and ice, as an apéritif.

Patras: a wine-growing region of the Peloponnese. It produces liqueur wines and white and rosé wines.

Peza: a wine-growing region of Crete. It produces red and white wines.

Phaskomilo: sage. This strongly aromatic herb combines well with such typically Mediterranean flavours as garlic, tomatoes and olive oil.

Phyllo: (also called fillo, filo): a type of wafer-thin puff pastry made from flour, salt and water. It is buttered and wrapped in multiple layers around sweet and savoury fillings.

Pittes: the general term for pies, pasties and flat loaves

Retsina: a very popular red, white or rosé wine, which gets its characteristic taste from the pine resin added during the fermentation process. Its harsh flavour is the perfect foil to the oiliness of Greek food. A particularly strong version is brewed in Greece's monasteries.

Revani: light, fluffy cakes soaked in sugar syrup; popular in northern Greece.

Rigani: oregano. It is used mostly dried for meat and vegetable dishes, and for sprinkling over salads and feta cheese.

Robola: a dry white wine from the Ionian Islands, especially Kefalonia

Rose water: a fragrant liquid derived from the essential oil distilled from rose petals. It is used to flavour and perfume confectionery.

Roux: a mixture of butter and flour used to thicken sauces. After the mixture has cooked gently, a liquid such as milk or stock is added to it to form the sauce.

Samos: an island off the Turkish coast famous for its pale golden Muscat dessert wine

Santorini: a volcanic island north of Crete that produces dry white wine and liqueur wine

Scarlet egg dye: a powder for dying the traditional hard-boiled Greek "Easter eggs". It is available from specialist Greek food shops. Any synthetic or natural food colouring can be used instead.

Sesame seeds: tiny black or white seeds from the sesame plant used for oil, paste and sweet dishes and pastries

Sitia: a wine-growing region on the eastern side of Crete. It produces full-bodied red and fruity liqueur wine.

Souvlakia: kebabs

Stifado: a Cretan stew made from braised beef and onions

sto fourno: baked in the oven

Tahini: a paste manufactured from ground sesame seeds. It is an ingredient in *hummus*.

Tapsi: type of versatile round roasting tin. It is used for baking the traditional Easter and New Year cakes.

Tarama (also known as *avgotarachon*): the coral-pink roe of the grey mullet; used to make *taramosalata*.

Taverna: a type of small, cheap eatery found all over Greece

Thimari: thyme. Fresh or dried leaves are used to season stews, meat and pasta.

Throumbes (also called *hamades*): ripe, black olives from the Aegean island of Samos

Tiganita: fried

Tyri: cheese

Trahana: cooked, dried and crushed wheat, sometimes blended with dried yogurt. It is often used as a soup base.

Tsakistes: variety of cracked green olives preserved in herbs and brine.

Tsipouro: a strong aperitif spirit distilled from fermented grapes after pressing. It is a speciality of northern Greece.

Tsirosalata: small, sun-dried young mackerel, seasoned with olive oil, lemon juice and dill

Vanilla-flavoured sugar: a flavoured sugar used in desserts, sold in jars or packets in some supermarkets and delicatessens. To make it at home, place a vanilla pod in a jar of caster sugar, close tightly and leave for a week or more; the longer it is left, the stronger the flavour.

Vasilikos: basil. This herb—its name in Greek means "royal"—is an essential ingredient in Mediterranean cuisine. Its strong flavour combines particularly well with tomato.

Vine leaves: the leaves of the grape vine, which grows throughout Greece, are edible and are used to wrap and to decorate food.

Yemista: stuffed

Yogurt: Greek yogurt, made from ewe's or—more commonly today—cow's milk, has a fat content of between 6 and 10 per cent. It is delicious served just with fresh fruit, a dribble of honey, and a sprinkling of nuts.

Zacharoplastio: a pastry shop

Agriohortasalata 30
Almond biscuits 126
Angel's hair rolls 130
Anginares me koukia 98
Anginares me spanaki 98
Arni me anginares 123
Arni sto fourno 110
Artichokes:
  and broad beans 98
  lamb with, 123
  and spinach bake 98
Athenian walnut cake 135
Aubergines:
  baked with eggs 70
  baked with meat 100
Avga matia melitzanes 70

Bakaliaros yiahni 88
Bamies laderes 103
Beans:
  pork and, 116
  in tomato sauce 28
Beefburgers with feta cheese 118
Beetroot salad 34
Bifteki me tiri 118
Black-eyed pea salad 36
Bonito:
  with vegetables 90
  with vegetables and olives (variation) 90
Bread: 120
    New Year (variation), 136
    plaited Easter, 136
    toasted, with cheese, onion and tomato topping 39
Briami 96
Broad beans, artichokes and, 98

Cabbage, carrot and egg salad 36
Cheese:
  fried, 40
  triangles 64
Chicken:
  with okra 111
  with olives 112
  soup with egg and lemon 48
Chick-pea soup 50
Country salad 35
Courgettes:
  fritters 28
  with egg and lemon sauce 104
  pie 63
Cream cheese:
  pasties 60
  pastries 126
Cretan pies, little, 63

CONVERSION CHART

These figures are not exact equivalents, but have been rounded up or down slightly to make measuring easier.

Weight Equivalents		Volume Equivalents	
Metric	Imperial	Metric	Imperial
15 g	½ oz	8 cl	3 fl oz
30 g	1 oz	12.5 cl	4 fl oz
60 g	2 oz	15 cl	¼ pint
90 g	3 oz	17.5 cl	6 fl oz
125 g	¼ lb	25 cl	8 fl oz
150 g	5 oz	30 cl	½ pint
200 g	7 oz	35 cl	12 fl oz
250 g	½ lb	45 cl	¾ pint
350 g	¾ lb	50 cl	16 fl oz
500 g	1 lb	60 cl	1 pint
1 kg	2 to 2¼ lb	1 litre	35 fl oz

Custard pie 132

Dako 39
Diples 128
Dolmades 44
Domates ke piperies yemistes 97

Eggs on a bed of vegetables 69

Fava 39
Fish:
  kebabs 87
  soup 53
Fish roe purée 33

Galaktobouriko 132
Garides giouvetsi 41
Gigantes plaki 28
Giouvetsi me kritharaki 74

Herbs 117
Hirino me gigantes 116
Hirino me selino 115
Honey 129
Horiatiki salata 35
Hylopittes metsovou 78

Kakavia 53
Kalamarakia tiganita 43
Kalamarakia yemisto 91
Kalizunia 126
Karidopitta Athinaiki 135
Kataifi me karidia 130
Katsikzaki che chimo porotkali 120
Kebabs:
  fish, 87
  lamb, 122
Keftedes me salsa domates 108
Kid in orange juice 120
Kolokithakia avgolemono 104
Kolokithakia keftedes 28
Kolokithobouriko 63
Kotopoulo me bamies 111
Kotopoulo me elies 112
Kotosoupa avgolemono 48
Koulouria 135
Kouneli me kamaki 118
Kourabiedes 126
Kreatopitta 58

Lachanosalata me karota 36
Lamb:
  with artichokes 123
  kebabs 122
  roast, 110
  stew with orzo pasta 74
Leeks:
  baked macaroni and, 76
  braised, 103

Lentil soup 48
Lithrini fourno ala spetsiota 82
"Little shoes" 104
Lovers' knots 128

Macaroni:
  baked, and leeks 76
  pie, meat and, 73
Meat:
  and macaroni pie 73
  pie 58
Meatballs in tomato sauce 108
Metsovo-style pasta squares 78
Midia me risi 73
Midia tiganita 33
Mitzithropittakia 60
Moscari me kidonia 115
Moussaka 100
Mussels:
  deep-fried, 33
  with rice 73

Octopus in wine 84
Okra:
  chicken with, 111
  in tomato sauce 103
Oktapodi krassato 84
Olives: 112
  chicken with, 112
Omeletta agriohorta 68
Omelette, wild vegetable, 68

Palamida plaki 90
Papoutsakia 104
Pasta: 75
  lamb stew with orzo, 74
  squares, metsovo-style, 78
Pastitsio 73
Pastitsio me prassa 76
Patsaria salata 34
Peasant soup 51
Peppers, baked sweet, 26
Phyllo 59
Piperies sto fourno 26
Pittes kritis 63
Pork:
  and beans 116
  ragout with celeriac 115
Potato and garlic purée 43
Prassa yiahni 103
Prawns, baked, 41

Quinces, veal with, 115

Rabbit in cream sauce 118
Revithia soupa 50
Rice:
  mussels with, 73
  spinach and, 76

Saganaki 40
Salata fassolia mavromatica 36
Salt cod:
  balls (variation) 88
  braised, 88
Sardelles sto fourno 92
Sardines:
  baked, 92
  fried (variation), 92
Sea bream: 83
  baked, 82
Sesame rings 135
Skordalia me patates 43
Smyrna sausages (variation) 108
Soupa fakes 48
Soupa horiatiki 51
Soupa trahana 53
Sour cherries in syrup 132
Souvlakia arniou 122
Souvlakia psaria 87
Souzoulakia smyrnaika (variation) 108
Spanakopitta 56
Spanakorizo 76
Spetsofai 69
Spinach:
  bake, artichoke and, 98
  pie 56
  and rice 76
Split-pea purée 39
Squid:
  deep-fried baby, 43
  stuffed, 91
Stifado 108
Swordfish, marinated, 87

Taramosalata 33
Tiropittakia 64
Trahana soup 53
Tsourekia 136
Tzatziki 27

Veal:
  braised, 108
  with quinces 115
Vegetable bake 96
Vegetables:
  bonito with, 90
  eggs on a bed of, 69
  stuffed, 97
Vine leaves, stuffed, 44
Vissino glyko 132

Wild vegetables: 30
  omelette 68
  salad 30

Xiphios marinatos 87

Yogurt with cucumber 27

Cover: *Dolmades,* vine leaves stuffed with a mixture of rice, onions, pine-nuts, currants and herbs (*recipe, page 44*) and *Horiatiki salata,* a country salad of raw tomatoes, cucumber, onions, olives, sweet peppers and feta cheese (*recipe, page 35*) make delicious *mezedes,* or appetizers. A bowl of black olives, crusty bread and a glass of wine complete the picture.

TIME
LIFE
BOOKS

TIME-LIFE BOOKS

COOKERY AROUND THE WORLD
English edition staff for *Greece*
Editorial: Ilse Gray, Luci Collings, Kate Cann
Production: Emma Wishart, Justina Cox
Technical Consultant: Michael A. Barnes

English translation by Isabel Varea for Ros Schwartz Translations, London

Published originally under the title *Küchen der Welt: Griechenland* by Gräfe und Unzer Verlag GmbH, Munich
© 1994 Gräfe und Unzer Verlag GmbH, Munich

This edition published by Time-Life Books B.V. Amsterdam
Authorized English language edition
© 1994 Time-Life Books B.V.
First English language printing 1994

ISBN 0 7054 1201 6

GRÄFE UND UNZER

EDITORS: Dr. Stephanie von Werz-Kovacs and Birgit Rademacker
Sub-Editor: Angela Hermann
Designer: Konstantin Kern
Stylist: Duan Osbar
Production:
BuchHaus.Kraxenberger.Gigler.GmbH
Cartography: Huber, Munich

Kristina Likidis-Königsfeld, the author, was born on the island of Crete and grew up in Athens before moving with her parents to the Rhineland. Now a freelance writer and journalist, based in Munich, her love for the cuisine of her homeland takes her back regularly to Greece in search of authentic regional dishes to extend her already impressive collection of Greek recipes.

Michael Brauner, who photographed the food for this volume, is a graduate of the Berlin Fotoschule. He worked as an assistant to several French and German photographers before setting up on his own in 1984. He now divides his time between his studios in Munich, Kalsruhe and Gordes in Provence.

Claudia Stöber lives in Wiesbaden, where she took a degree in graphic design and illustration. A freelancer working for publishers and advertising agencies, she uses a varied range of styles and materials, but has a particular preferences for water colours and landscape painting, as shown in the illustrations for this book.

Picture Credits

Colour illustrations: Claudia Stöber

All photographs were taken by Michael Brauner, Food Fotografie, unless indicated below.

Cover: Graham Kirk, London. 4 (Byzantine church, Monemvasia, Peloponnes, top left): Martin Thomas, Aachen. 4 (windmills in Mykonos, top centre; church on Ios, bottom left): Thomas Stankiewicz, Munich. 4 (Temple of Apollo and rock of Acro-Corinth, Peloponnese, centre left; woman winding wool, Karpathos, bottom centre): Bildagentur J. Dziemballa, Dr. Janicke, Munich. 5 (statues, Temple of Hera, near Pythagorio, top; fisherman on Skiathos, bottom): Martin Thomas, Aachen. 8-9 (church on Santorini): Bildagentur J. Dziemballa, Dr. Janicke, Munich. 10, 11 (2): Gerhard P. Müller, Dortmund. 12, 13: Herann Rademaker, Munich. 14 (2), 15: Photo & Presse Franz Roth, Nuremberg. 16 (2): Martin Thomas, Aachen. 17 top: Thomas Stankiewicz, Munich. 17 bottom: Bildagentur J. Dziemballa, Dr. Janicke, Munich. 18: Martin Thomas, Aachen. 19 (2): Gerhard P. Müller, Dortmund. 20: Herbert Hartmann, Munich. 21 top: Thomas Stankiewicz, Munich. 21 bottom: Martin Thomas, Aachen. 22: Bildagentur J. Dziemballa, Dr. Janicke, Munich. 23 top: Gerhard P. Müller, Dortmund. 23 bottom, 30, 112: Taneli Türkkan, Bernried. 120: Erich Raab, Munich.

Colour reproduction by Fotolito Longo, Bolzano, Italy
Typeset by A. J. Latham Limited, Dunstable, Bedfordshire, England
Printed and bound by Mondadori, Verona, Italy